Conclave

FADE IN:

EXT. APARTMENT BLOCK - ROME - NIGHT

A large, modern apartment block in a modest part of the city. The streets are quiet. Everyone sleeps.

INT. APARTMENT - ROME - NIGHT

CLOSE on a WINDOW PANE, small, leaded. We HOLD on the glass, nothing but black night outside, not sure what we're supposed to be looking at.

Then, with a sharp *ping*, the pane cracks.

ON A SLEEPING MAN, his back to us. Woken by the sound, the man raises his head from the pillow, stares at the cracked pane.

Silence.

The sudden jangle of a phone in the room. The man turns his head to stare at the phone.

EXT. TUNNEL NEAR VATICAN - ROME - NIGHT

CLOSE - PUSHING the MAN as he walks quickly through a tunnel, his sleep-whorled hair standing in undignified tufts from the back of his head. A lone car passes.

EXT. STREET NEAR VATICAN - ROME - NIGHT

The MAN continues to rush through the empty streets. The only sound is his heavy breathing and footsteps. Ahead of him a blue light pulses in SOFT FOCUS against the vague bulk of St Peter's.

I/E. SHOP - STREET NEAR VATICAN - NIGHT

Outside on the street the MAN passes a SHOP WINDOW and for a moment we hold on the display - rows of PLASTIC PIETÀS.

OMITTED

OMITTED

OMITTED

INT. CASA SANTA MARTA - LIFT PAPAL CORRIDOR - NIGHT

In the lift the MAN - CARDINAL LAWRENCE - stares down at his hand and realises he is clutching his red *zucchetto*. We are still on his back as he smoothes down his hair and puts it on his head. Then he turns to the mirror <u>and we see his face for the first time: careworn, anonymous. An administrator.</u>

Lawrence glances at his ashen reflection in the mirrored walls, looks away. The elevator arrives. Lawrence raises his chin, prepares his public face. The doors slide open to reveal a solid wall of MEN IN BLACK SUITS.

INT. CASA SANTA MARTA - PAPAL CORRIDOR - NIGHT

The wall of SECURITY parts with difficulty and he makes his way through them towards the Papal Suite. White marbled floors. It could be a hotel, a clinic.

ARCHBISHOP WOZNIAK, built like a labourer, eyes, behind his glasses, red from crying, comes to meet him.

ARCHBISHOP WOZNIAK
(Helplessly)
Eminence...

Lawrence takes his cheeks in his hand.

LAWRENCE
Janusz, your presence made him so happy.

Ahead of them a BODYGUARD steps aside and Lawrence walks on into...

INT. PAPAL SUITE - NIGHT

Lawrence stops, surprised by the throng of people crowded into the little living room. He realises with a faint stab of pain, that he must have been one of the last summoned. He follows Wozniak through the open doors into...

INT. PAPAL BEDROOM - NIGHT

The room is almost shockingly plain - a chest of drawers, nightstand, an anonymous bed that could be found in any hotel. And lying on this bed, slightly propped up on pillows, lies the dead Pope.

Kneeling around the bed are the three other senior cardinals of the Catholic Church: ALDO BELLINI, JOSEPH TREMBLAY, JOSHUA ADEYEMI.

The room is so small he has to step over the backs of their legs to reach the head of the bed.

He stares down at the Pope, the expression of almost wry amusement on the dead man's face.

ADEYEMI
Subvenite, Sancti Dei...

Lawrence realises they have been waiting for him to begin the liturgy and hurriedly kneels, joints creaking. He glances back at the sitting room beyond. Everyone is kneeling, head bowed. He buries his face in his hands as the Nigerian cardinal's deep voice reverberates in the tiny room.

ADEYEMI (CONT'D)
... occurrite, Angeli Domini,
Suscipientes animam eius.
Offerentes eam in conspectu
Altissimi...

ALL CARDINALS
Suscipiat te Christus qui vocavit te
et in sinum Abrahae angeli deducant
te.

As the prayer continues Lawrence half-opens his eyes. His gaze wanders around the scene before him, as if still trying to comprehend what has happened...

...the folded spectacles on the bedside table, the scuffed alarm clock beside them, the simple crucifix above the bed...

A heart-breaking detail: the wooden rim of the headboard is cracked, the padded panel within, fraying...

Finally the familiar face, strangely naked without the customary spectacles...

He realises Adeyemi has finished. The Cardinals recite the chorus.

ALL CARDINALS (CONT'D)
Sicut erat in principio et nunc et
semper et in saecula saeculorum.
Amen.

For a few moments the room is completely still. Then...

TREMBLAY
He is with God.

The Canadian Tremblay, *Carmerlengo* or Chamberlain - silver hair immaculately coiffed, the trim build of a retired athlete - stretches out his arms as if in blessing. Two ASSISTANTS hurry forward and help him up. Lawrence rises creakily to his feet with the other Cardinals.

TREMBLAY (CONT'D)
Archbishop Wozniak.

Wozniak edges around the bed and, sweating with embarrassment, struggles to pull a RING from the Pope's hand. Finally he works it free and presents it to Tremblay who produces a pair of shears from a silver box. Grimacing with effort he cuts free the metal disc of St Peter from the ring. The snap is audible in the silent room.

TREMBLAY (CONT'D)
Sede vacante. The throne of the Holy See is vacant.

INT. PAPAL SUITE - NIGHT

Groups of dignitaries stand in whispered conference. Lawrence gingerly works his way through the throng to a lone figure standing by the desk: the lean, ascetic frame of his friend, Cardinal Bellini, Secretary of State.

LAWRENCE
(Joining him)
Aldo...

Bellini is staring down at a little plastic travel CHESS SET on the desk - almost the only personal item in the bland room. He brushes the pieces, grouped mid-game, with a finger.

BELLINI
Do you think anyone would mind if I took this, Thomas? As a keepsake?

LAWRENCE
Of course. Take it. He would have wanted you to have it.

BELLINI
We used to play quite often at the end of the day. He said it helped him relax.

LAWRENCE
Who won?

BELLINI
Oh, he did. Always eight moves ahead.

His eyes suddenly fill with tears. Moved, Lawrence takes his arm.

LAWRENCE
Ah, Aldo, I'm so sorry. What happened, do you know?

BELLINI
They say heart attack. There had been warnings.

Lawrence blinks in surprise.

LAWRENCE
I hadn't heard that.

BELLINI
He didn't want anyone to know. He thought if word got out *they* would start spreading rumours he was going to resign.

Lawrence is trying not to show his hurt at being excluded. Bellini mistakes his silence for puzzlement.

BELLINI (CONT'D)
(Quietly)
The *Curia*.

Lawrence nods, rouses himself to action. Tremblay, across the room, is watching.

LAWRENCE
We'll have to be careful what we say to the media about his condition.

INT. PAPAL SUITE - SITTING ROOM - NIGHT

Lawrence and Bellini find Wozniak sitting alone in the dark. Lawrence addresses him gently.

LAWRENCE
Janusz, I know this is hard for you, but we'll need to prepare a detailed statement. Who discovered the Holy Father's body?

ARCHBISHOP WOZNIAK
I did, Your Eminence.

LAWRENCE
Well, thank God, that's something. What did you do?

ARCHBISHOP WOZNIAK
I called the Holy Father's doctor. He always spent the night in the room next door. But... it was too late.

LAWRENCE
What time was this?

ARCHBISHOP WOZNIAK
Around eleven thirty, Eminence.
(Off Thomas' surprise)
I would have called you sooner, but...

Wozniak shrugs helplessly. Tremblay arrives just in time at the door.

TREMBLAY
Thomas, I'm so sorry. I know His Holiness had no closer colleagues than you and Aldo... But I asked Janusz to hold off calling you. I... I wanted to ascertain all the facts.

LAWRENCE
Well, I'm sure you acted for the best.

TREMBLAY
(walking towards them)
The way rumours can spread. One and a quarter billion souls watching.

He draws a document from his cassock. Bellini sits down next to Wozniak.

TREMBLAY (CONT'D)
I've prepared a time-line of His Holiness' last day.

Lawrence examines it. He suddenly feels the bulk of Adeyemi, *Cardinal Major Penitentiary* or confessor-in-chief - at his shoulder. Tremblay passes them more sheets.

TREMBLAY (CONT'D)
The Holy Father's most recent medical records. He had an angiogram last month.

Lawrence is holding the x-ray to the light, staring in silence, <u>struck that he is looking at the very heart of the man he revered</u>.

TREMBLAY (CONT'D)
(Pointing)
You can see the evidence of a blockage...just *here*.

Lawrence and Bellini share a look - a flinch of distress.

LAWRENCE
Joe, perhaps...perhaps we could release the data, but not the photograph? It feels too...too....

Tremblay inclines his head sympathetically.

TREMBLAY
I know, Thomas, I know. But there *will* have to be an autopsy.

Adeyemi is still scanning the time-line.

ADEYEMI
The time before Vespers? What was he doing then?

TREMBLAY
Routine meetings as far as I understand it.

ADEYEMI
Who was the last to have a scheduled meeting with him?

TREMBLAY
I believe that may have been me. I saw him at four. Is that right Janusz? Was I the last?

ARCHBISHOP WOZNIAK
You were, Eminence.

ADEYEMI
Put in all the meetings he had that day. It will show how hard he was working, right up to the end.

TREMBLAY
That might look as if we were placing a huge burden on a sick man.

ADEYEMI
The Papacy is a huge burden. Especially for an older man.

Silence. A slight tension. Adeyemi is the youngest here. The contest has begun. Lawrence breaks the awkward silence.

LAWRENCE
Has anyone telephoned Cardinal Tedesco?

Bellini straightens and for the first time we see that beneath the grief there is a well of anger.

LAWRENCE (CONT'D)
As a courtesy.

BELLINI
Courtesy? What has he ever done to deserve courtesy? If anyone can be said to have killed the Holy Father, he did!

LAWRENCE
I have to ring him, Aldo.

INT. PAPAL OFFICE - NIGHT

Lawrence steps through the open door of the SMALL OFFICE and dials the desk phone.

LAWRENCE
(Italian, To Operator)
< The Patriarch's Palace in Venice, please. Cardinal Tedesco's private line. >

LAWRENCE
(To Operator)
Il Palazzo Patriarcale di Venezia, per favore. La linea privata del cardinale Tedesco.

After a moment.

TEDESCO (O.S.)
(Over phone)
Tedesco.

LAWRENCE
(Italian)
< Goffredo? It's Lawrence. I'm afraid I have terrible news. The Holy Father has just passed away.>

LAWRENCE
Goffredo? Sono Lawrence. Purtroppo devo comunicarvi una terribile notizia. Il Santo Padre è appena deceduto.

Lawrence listens to the phone. Silence. The sound of movement, a door closing?

LAWRENCE (CONT'D)
(Italian)
< Your Eminence? >

LAWRENCE (CONT'D)
Eminenza?

TEDESCO (O.S.)
(Beat, Italian)
< Thank you, Lawrence. I shall pray for his soul. >

TEDESCO (O.S.)
(Beat)
Grazie, Lawrence. Pregherò per la sua anima.

He hangs up. The others watch from the doorway.

LAWRENCE
He already knew.

Tremblay takes out what appears to be a small leather bound prayer book - but turns out to be a mobile phone.

BELLINI
Of course he knew. This place is full of his supporters. He probably knew before we did.

TREMBLAY
(Checking his phone)
It's trending.
(Off the stares of the others)
The rumours that the Pope is dead are trending.
(A further, smiling, explanation)
On the *internet*. We should move quickly or we'll fall behind the news cycle.

ADEYEMI
We should wait until daylight. The dignity of the office requires...

BELLINI
For God's sake, Joshua. When did the Holy Father ever care about the "dignity of the office?" Look at his rooms.

TREMBLAY
The body should be embalmed. Remember Pius XII? Went off like a firecracker in his coffin...

Lawrence jumps slightly as Adeyemi addresses him.

ADEYEMI
Well, Dean. The responsibility for the Conclave falls upon you.

Lawrence looks up and finds the others staring at him. The dawning realisation of what lies ahead.

INT. PAPAL SUITE - BEDROOM - NIGHT

Lawrence stands, watching WOZNIAK laying a thin white VEIL over the dead Pope's face. He turns to the PRIESTS of the Apostolic Camera, standing waiting.

LAWRENCE
(Italian)
< *Seal the room.* >

LAWRENCE
Sigillate la stanza.

TITLES BEGIN

The Pope's body is zipped into a a semi-transparent white body bag and heaved onto a gurney. Lawrence watches as it is being wheeled out into the corridor.

The sealing of the suite begins. The door is locked. Red tape is fixed on the frame. Wozniak is looking on.

Lawrence stands in the lift. From his place at the bottom of the gurney, he stares fixedly down at the feet of the Pope, ghostly through the white plastic, curled like small foetuses.

The elevator pings and the doors slide open...

The gurney with the dead Pope is wheeled through the UNDERGROUND GARAGE, past a puddle of oil...a crushed cigarette pack...

The only sound is the faint squeal of the wheels, and, the forbidden click of phone cameras...

The sealing of the door continues - the tape criss-crossing backwards and forwards, as if this was a crime-scene...

Wax seals bearing the coat of arms of the *Cardinal Camerlengo* fix the tape ends to the frame....

Outside the body is loaded into the waiting ambulance....

The final wax seal is put in place...

...as the ambulance drives off, the dead Pope in the body bag inside.

FADE OUT

TITLE CARD: THREE WEEKS LATER. SUNDAY, 7TH NOVEMBER, EVE OF CONCLAVE.

FADE IN

INT/EXT. CASA SANTA MARTA - FACADE - MORNING

WORKMEN are fitting electronic SHUTTERS over the windows. The whine of power tools as screws are tightened into place.

INT. CASA SANTA MARTA - BEDROOM - MORNING

Inside the Casa a WORKMAN tests the closing of the shutters with a remote control. It works.

INT. CASA SANTA MARTA - CORRIDOR - MORNING

More Workmen emerge from the bedrooms, each trundling a dolly loaded with the TELEVISIONS being removed from the rooms.

INT. SISTINE CHAPEL - MORNING

A SPIRAL PATTERN...

Intricate and beautiful. A mosaic floor. As we watch a wide red carpet is rolled across the frame, obscuring the mosaic. An easy-lift rises in front of the last judgement.

CLOSE ON LAWRENCE'S FACE

...looking up. As we watch, a SHADOW falls over his face.

Above him, metal panels are being fitted over the high windows, shutting out the daylight, <u>obscuring the ceiling in near gloom</u>.

Lawrence stands in the chapel, watching the sealing of the windows unhappily.

All around him there is teeming activity. Behind him WORKMEN hurriedly finish laying the temporary wooden floor. At the other end of the chapel carpet is being rolled over the wood, followed by the *thunk* of a nail gun.

ARCHBISHOP MANDORFF, Master of Papal Liturgical Celebrations, (60's, German), stands beside him, clipboard in hand.

ARCHBISHOP MANDORFF
Security say they'd like to test the electronic jammers one last time, your Eminence.

LAWRENCE
Then they'd better be quick.
(Of the windows)
Is this really necessary, Willi?

ARCHBISHOP MANDORFF
Apparently so. Security say...
(reading, slightly mystified)
...eavesdroppers can use lasers to "read the vibrations on the glass?"

LAWRENCE
Let's hope none of our brothers suffer from claustrophobia. Who knows how long we'll have to be in here.

Lawrence stares around him at the chaos.

LAWRENCE (CONT'D)
(shouting over the racket)
I assume we *are* going to finish in time?

ARCHBISHOP MANDORFF
They will work through the night if they have to. It will be fine, Eminence. It always is. Italy, you know.

Lawrence nods, pats the German's arm.

LAWRENCE
Sorry to fuss.

He walks to one of the long tables along the length of the chapel. On it Monsignor O' Malley and some assistants are setting up Bible, prayer book, pens and pencils, a ballot paper and long list of names of the 107 cardinals eligible to vote for the next Pope.

MONSIGNOR O'MALLEY, Secretary of the College of Cardinals, (Irish, 40's) joins them.

MONSIGNOR O'MALLEY
Well, Eminence, I'd say this is a pretty fair vision of hell.

LAWRENCE
Don't be blasphemous, Ray. Hell arrives tomorrow when we bring in the cardinals.

He examines the list of names.

LAWRENCE (CONT'D)
(Of a name)
How on earth does one pronounce this? Salso?

ARCHBISHOP MANDORFF
Kahl-koh, Eminence. He's Indian.

LAWRENCE
Kahl-koh. Thank you Willi.

He sits, testing the cushion, wondering if it will offer comfort for the elderly men who will soon be using them.

MONSIGNOR O'MALLEY
Archbishop Wozniak has asked if he may have a word, Eminence?

Lawrence stands again, prods the cushion.

LAWRENCE
I don't think that's possible. The cardinals will begin arriving in an hour. What's it about?

MONSIGNOR O'MALLEY
He didn't say. (Beat). I wouldn't have mentioned it but he seemed so...upset?

Lawrence frowns at him.

LAWRENCE
We're going to be sequestered from six o'clock. He should have come earlier.

MONSIGNOR O'MALLEY
Yes, your Eminence. I'll tell him.

He starts to leave. Lawrence considers.

LAWRENCE
Ray? Tell him I'll see him after I've met the cardinals. The poor fellow will be worrying about his future.

O'Malley nods and leaves.

LAWRENCE (CONT'D)
(Wryly)
Getting puffed up with my own importance, Willi.

He holds out a hand for Mandorff to help him stand.

LAWRENCE (CONT'D)
(Rising with a wince)
The Conclave will be over in a few days and then no-one will be interested in me.

A DRILL starts nearby, the sound deafening in the chapel. Lawrence winces, feels a headache coming on.

INT. SISTINE CHAPEL - ANTECHAMBER - MORNING

Behind the altar of the chapel Lawrence descends a set of stairs. He crosses a narrow sacristy to descend into a small room.

INT. SISTINE CHAPEL - ROOM OF TEARS - MORNING

Lawrence closes the door, muffling the sound of the work beyond. He stands for a moment, savouring the relative peace. He finds himself staring at the THRONE, on which the newly-elected Pontiff will sit. He crosses to a clothes rail and brushes a hand along the row of cellophane wrapped papal cassocks.

The door opens and Bellini slips in, closing the door behind him.

BELLINI
Shelter from the Storm.

Lawrence smiles, examines one of the cassocks.

BELLINI (CONT'D)
Dear Lord, that's enormous.

LAWRENCE
Apparently Pope John the Twenty-Third was too fat to fit into the biggest cassock. They had to split the seam in the back for him to get into it.

He picks up a pair of shoes, slip-ons in red leather.

BELLINI
You look tired.

LAWRENCE
All this... it's a duty I never thought I'd have to perform.
(Beat)
I always assumed he would out-live us all.

To his surprise he finds himself continuing....

LAWRENCE (CONT'D)
We... we didn't part well.

He stares at the shoes to avoid Bellini's gaze.

LAWRENCE (CONT'D)
I asked for his permission to retire as Dean. Join an order. I have been having... difficulties.

BELLINI
(Beat)
What did he say?

LAWRENCE
He refused my resignation. Said that some were chosen to be Shepherds, and some to manage the farm. Apparently, I'm a manager.

He gives Bellini a crooked, painful smile.

LAWRENCE (CONT'D)
Things were a little cold between us when I left. (Beat). And that was the last time I saw him.

Bellini hesitates. Then...

BELLINI
The Holy Father told me of your... crisis of faith. He said you had difficulties with prayer.

Lawrence feels shocked, obscurely betrayed.

BELLINI (CONT'D)
You know that he had doubts himself, by the end?

LAWRENCE
The Pope had doubts about God?

BELLINI
Never about God. What he had lost faith in was the Church.

The two friends stare at each other.

I/E. MINIBUS - MORNING

A group of NUNS, wearing blue habit, sit on a minibus, the walls of the Vatican outside the window. In their midst a woman with an aristocratic air - SISTER AGNES.

EXT. CASA SANTA MARTA - PARKING - MORNING

As the buses park inside the Vatican the NUNS descend and walk up to the Casa.

INT. CASA SANTA MARTA - LOBBY - DAY

The line of NUNS are entering the building.

INT. CASA SANTA MARTA - BACK OFFICE - DAY

Sister Agnes arrives in her office. She puts down her bag and takes off her coat, glances at the plan for the day. In the corner a canary in a cage. Sister Agnes walks over and feeds it.

EXT. CASA SANTA MARTA - COURTYARD - DAY

Lawrence stands, wrapped in a winter coat against the cold, on the steps of the Casa, staring up at the sky. He is flanked again by O'Malley and Mandorff, other members of staff hovering beside them. For a moment LAWRENCE listens to the faint sound of thousands of voices outside on the streets, drums echoing.

ARCHBISHOP MANDORFF
Here they come, Your Eminence.

He's talking about the group of cardinals who are now passing the gate into the courtyard, crossing towards him. They are accompanied by two Security Guards, and the clatter of their wheeled suitcases. As they approach Lawrence opens his arms.

LAWRENCE
Brothers, welcome.

CARDINAL MENDOZA
Are we criminals now? Searched? Luggage opened...

LAWRENCE
(Taking his hands)
I'm so sorry, Your Eminence, but we are told there is a heightened state of security.

CARDINAL MENDOZA shows Lawrence his sleeve.

CARDINAL MENDOZA
(In disgust)
And look at this. Spat upon. The Protestors. We're *all* paedophiles now, apparently.
(Dropping his voice)
Don Tutino?

LAWRENCE
(Quietly)
Will *not* be attending.

Mendoza nods grimly and walks on.

EXT. CASA SANTA MARTA - COURTYARD - LATER

In MONTAGE we see further arrivals: The Africans led by the magisterial Adeyemi, pointing out this building and that to his party, like a proprietor. From the Eastern Ministries, the Archbishops of Lebanon and Antioch. From India the Archbishops of Trivandrum, Ernakulam-Angamaly and...

LAWRENCE
(Pronouncing carefully)
Eminence *Khal-Koh*, welcome!

Lawrence shakes his hand in the staircase.

Back in the courtyard Tremblay arrives at the same time as the over-weight CARDINAL GUTTOSO. He has his choir dress in a dry-cleaning bag slung over his shoulder, a Nike sports bag swinging in the other. He raises both hands to indicate he cannot shake.

TREMBLAY
Thomas!

Guttoso, in contrast has an assistant struggling behind him with his three, huge cases. As he waddles past Lawrence and Tremblay exchange a look.

TREMBLAY (CONT'D)
(Of the cases)
Is he smuggling in his private Chef?

EXT. CASA SANTA MARTA - COURTYARD - AFTERNOON

THE SKY -- the drone of a helicopter, either security or media, hidden from our sight by the low cloud cover.

ON LAWRENCE

...staring up at the clouds, listening to the sinister hum. He turns back to Mandorff and O'Malley who are waiting with him in the cold. It's getting dark now.

LAWRENCE
How many is that, Willi?

ARCHBISHOP MANDORFF
One hundred and three, Eminence.

LAWRENCE
I wonder where Tedesco has got to.

MONSIGNOR O'MALLEY
Perhaps he isn't coming?

LAWRENCE
That would be too much to hope for.

MONSIGNOR O'MALLEY
(Of the cold)
We can wait inside if you prefer?

LAWRENCE
No, let's get some fresh air while we still can.

He notices Bellini striding towards them and descends the steps to greet his friend.

BELLINI
Am I the last?

LAWRENCE
Not quite. How are you?

BELLINI
Oh fairly dreadful. You've seen the papers? Apparently it's already decided it's to be me.

LAWRENCE
And I happen to agree with them.

BELLINI
What if I don't want it? No sane man would want the papacy.

LAWRENCE
Some of our colleagues seem to.

BELLINI
But what if I know in my heart I'm not worthy?

LAWRENCE
You're more worthy than any of us.

BELLINI
I'm not.

LAWRENCE
Then... tell your supporters not to vote for you. Pass the chalice...

Bellini looks past him, his expression hardening.

BELLINI
And let it go to him? How am I to live with myself if I don't try to stop him?

He walks towards the Casa Santa Marta as Lawrence turns to face the newcomer: TEDESCO, the Patriarch of Venice. He looks like a retired butcher, broken-nosed, the physique of a bull.

TEDESCO
< Apologies, Lawrence. My train was delayed in Venice.>

TEDESCO
Chiedo scusa, Lawrence. Il mio treno era in ritardo a Venezia.

LAWRENCE
(Italian)
< Father Tedesco. We've missed you. >

LAWRENCE
Padre Tedesco. Ci siete mancato.

Tedesco laughs.

TEDESCO
(Italian)
< No doubt. But don't worry, my friends have kept me well informed. >

TEDESCO
Non c'è dubbio. Ma non preoccupatevi, i miei amici - how do you say *- mi hanno tenuto ben informato.*

Lawrence, refusing to be goaded, keeps his smile in place.

LAWRENCE
(Italian)
< Are you well? >

LAWRENCE
State bene?

TEDESCO
(Italian)
< Ah, no-one is ever well at our age. How have you found your new responsibilities? You have everything under control? >

TEDESCO
Ah, no-one is ever well at our age. Come vi trovate con le vostre nuove responsabilità? Avete tutto sotto controllo?

LAWRENCE
< I believe so. >

LAWRENCE
Credo di sì.

TEDESCO
< Good. >
(To a waiting assistant)
< Stop hovering. I carry my own bag. >

TEDESCO
Bene.
(a un assistente)
Smettetela di stare in agguato. La porto io la mia borsa.

Lawrence watches him stump on to the entrance. He offers up a quiet prayer.

LAWRENCE
Heavenly Father, Bless this Conclave, and guide it in Wisdom.

From above the drone of the helicopter is heard again.

INT. CASA SANTA MARTA - BEDROOMS - EVENING

The NUNS glide silently around the rooms. Beds are turned down, pillows smoothed.

INT. CASA SANTA MARTA - BATHROOM - EVENING

Little packets of toiletries are placed by the NUNS.

OMITTED

INT. CASA SANTA MARTA - SECURITY GATE - EVENING

The surreal sight of cardinals handing in their mobile phones at reception, queueing to pass through a METAL DETECTOR. Sister Agnes watches over the process.

SISTER AGNES
(Italian)
< *The iPad too, your Eminence.* >

SISTER AGNES
Anche l'iPad, Eminenza.

INT. CASA SANTA MARTA - STORAGE ROOM - EVENING

A NUN is placing the confiscated MOBILE PHONES and devices into dockets, each in a labelled plastic bag.

INT. CASA SANTA MARTA - HALLWAY - EVENING

Lawrence walks quickly with Monsignor O'Malley, both trailed by the young chaplain, FATHER HAAS.

LAWRENCE
(Impatient)
Where is he?

O'MALLEY
The meeting room, Your Eminence.

LAWRENCE *
(handing coat and scarf to Haas; Italian)
Will you take these upstairs for me?

LAWRENCE
Me li porta di sopra, per favore?

O'MALLEY
Do you want me to sit in?

LAWRENCE
No, no, I'll deal with it.

INT. CASA SANTA MARTA - MEETING ROOM - EVENING

He opens the door to the room and finds Wozniak with his back to him at the far end of the room, staring at the wall.

LAWRENCE
(Closing the door after him)
Janusz?

Wozniak turns, looking ashen. He's been drinking. He sinks to his knees, makes the sign of the cross.

ARCHBISHOP WOZNIAK
In the name of the Father, the Son and the Holy Ghost. My last confession was four weeks ago...

Lawrence walks to him, a little irritated.

LAWRENCE
(Helping him up)
Janusz, Janusz, I'm sorry I don't have *time* to hear your confession. There is so much still to do.

Wozniak sinks into a chair. Wipes sweat from his face with trembling hands. Lawrence examines him in surprise.

LAWRENCE (CONT'D)
Have you been drinking?

Wozniak looks at him, wretched. Lawrence sighs inwardly.

LAWRENCE (CONT'D)
What's troubling you? Tell me.

ARCHBISHOP WOZNIAK
I should have come to you before. But I promised I wouldn't say anything.

LAWRENCE
Promised who?

ARCHBISHOP WOZNIAK
Cardinal Tremblay.

Lawrence feels an instinctive stab of alarm, his natural aversion to secrets. Almost without realising it, he is drifting back towards the door.

LAWRENCE
Janusz, the doors close soon and you'll have to leave. Now if you promised Father Tremblay then perhaps it isn't right for you to...

ARCHBISHOP WOZNIAK
(Blurting)
The day the Pope died, the last person to have an official appointment with him was Cardinal Tremblay.

LAWRENCE
(Impatient)
Yes, I know. It's on the official timeline for...

ARCHBISHOP WOZNIAK
At that meeting, the Holy Father dismissed him from all his offices in the Church.

That stops Lawrence in his tracks.

LAWRENCE
What?

ARCHBISHOP WOZNIAK
He sacked him.

Lawrence stares at him. He starts to speak, stops, dimly aware that he feels anger - *anger at being burdened with this*.

LAWRENCE
(Tight)
Why?

ARCHBISHOP WOZNIAK
For gross misconduct.

Lawrence stares at him, staggered.

LAWRENCE
You...you tell me this *now?* We are about to be sequestered and...

ARCHBISHOP WOZNIAK
Forgive me! But it wasn't until the last few days, when I started to hear the rumours...

LAWRENCE
(Sharply)
What rumours?

ARCHBISHOP WOZNIAK
That he might be elected Pope.

LAWRENCE
And you see it as your duty to *prevent* that, do you?

ARCHBISHOP WOZNIAK
I no longer know what my duty is.

It's said with such obvious sincerity, such *misery*, that Lawrence feels ashamed of his anger. He sits.

LAWRENCE
(Beat)
Were you there at this meeting?

ARCHBISHOP WOZNIAK
No, Your Eminence. The Holy Father told me about it afterwards, when we had supper.

LAWRENCE
Did he tell you *why* he had dismissed Father Tremblay?

ARCHBISHOP WOZNIAK
No. He said the reasons would become clear soon enough. He was very angry.

Lawrence feels a brief flare of hope that he could be lying, but dismisses it quickly.

LAWRENCE
Does anyone else know about this?

ARCHBISHOP WOZNIAK
Monsignor Morales was at the meeting.

LAWRENCE
Why hasn't he mentioned anything to me? He was there in the apartment with us the night the Holy Father died.

ARCHBISHOP WOZNIAK
(Tearing up)
After the Holy Father... after ...
(unable to say it)
I went to see Monsignor Morales to tell him what the Pope had said but he was very firm. He said there had been no dismissal and that the Holy Father had not been his usual self in the last weeks. He said I shouldn't raise the subject again. But... it's not right, Eminence. God tells me it's not right.

Lawrence stands, pained, one word in his mind. *Scandal.*

OMITTED

INT. CASA SANTA MARTA - LOBBY - NIGHT

Only the ground floor is now lit, like an aquarium. Lawrence stands at the entrance in the green light, watching Wozniak as he walks away. Wozniak raises a hand in awkward farewell then walks on, as shutters rattle their way down over the windows, shutting out the world. A SECURITY GUARD closes and locks the main door.

It is beginning.

INT. CASA SANTA MARTA - KITCHENS - NIGHT

The kitchen is crowded with NUNS busy preparing the evening meal for the 107 cardinals. Despite their number, the atmosphere is hushed, each focussed on her task.

INT. CASA SANTA MARTA - DINING ROOM - NIGHT

The NUNS are laying the tables for the evening meal.

SISTER AGNES inspects the placement of the silverware, correcting it with military precision.

INT. CASA SANTA MARTA - STAIRCASE - NIGHT

Lawrence is walking up the stairs, eager to get to his room. Behind him O'Malley calls out from reception.

MONSIGNOR O'MALLEY
Your Eminence...

O'Malley hurries over. The usually cheerful Irishman looks disconcerted. He hesitates.

LAWRENCE
Oh dear God, one of them's died.

MONSIGNOR O'MALLEY
What?

LAWRENCE
Have we lost a Cardinal?

MONSIGNOR O'MALLEY
No, Your Eminence. We seem to have acquired one.
(Off Lawrence's stern face)
I mean it literally, Eminence. Another cardinal has just turned up.

Lawrence stares at him. The day is turning into a nightmare. O'Malley leads him up the staircase.

LAWRENCE
If we've left someone off the list...

MONSIGNOR O'MALLEY
He was never *on* our lists. He says he was created *in pectore*.

LAWRENCE
(Beat)
He has to be an imposter, surely?

MONSIGNOR O'MALLEY
That's what I thought, Eminence. But Archbishop Mandorff has spoken to him and thinks not.

O'Malley guides him up the stairs towards Mandorff who stands with two NUNS. They take in his expression and quickly glide away.

LAWRENCE
What's this I'm hearing?

ARCHBISHOP MANDORFF
(Shaken)
His name is Vincent Benitez, Eminence. He's the Archbishop of Kabul.

Lawrence almost double-takes.

LAWRENCE
Archbishop of *where?*

ARCHBISHOP MANDORFF
Kabul. He's Mexican. The Holy Father appointed him last year.

LAWRENCE
Last year? And how has this been kept a secret?

ARCHBISHOP MANDORFF
I thought, perhaps, you would be aware of his elevation.

LAWRENCE
No. I am not.

He feels the nervous gazes of the others on him and gets control of himself.

LAWRENCE (CONT'D)
Ray, ask Father Bellini to join us. Perhaps he knew of this.

O'Malley hurries off.

ARCHBISHOP MANDORFF
He has a letter of appointment from the Pope addressed to the archdiocese of Kabul, which they kept secret at the Holy Father's request.
(Beat)
You don't think he could have forged it?

Lawrence sighs.

LAWRENCE
Where is he now?

INT. CASA SANTA MARTA - KITCHEN STORAGE - NIGHT

We're looking at a slim man dressed in a somewhat shabby plain black attire with no skull cap. This is BENITEZ. He sits on a plastic chair, rosary in hand.

Lawrence, Bellini, Mandorff and O'Malley watch him through the glass wall of the room.

BELLINI
A cardinal in Afghanistan? It's absurd. How many catholics <u>are</u> there in Afghanistan?

Lawrence gestures to the LETTER he's holding.

LAWRENCE
He was the Head of the Catholic Mission there until his... elevation.

BELLINI
The Americans will be appalled. How could we possibly ensure his safety?

LAWRENCE
Presumably that's why the Holy Father wanted it kept secret.
(Beat)
Well it won't be *in pectore* now. I don't think we have any choice but to admit him.

He moves to enter the office but Bellini takes his arm. He stops, turns to Bellini, who seems as surprised as him at his intervention. For a moment the Italian continues to stare at the newcomer. It's as if there's something about Benitez that Bellini finds obscurely troubling. Then...

BELLINI
(Quietly)
Must we?
(Off Thomas' puzzled look)
Are we *sure* the Holy Father was entirely... *competent* to make this appointment?

Lawrence stares at him, thinking back to Wozniak's words, tempted by the explanation of mental confusion... Bellini misreads the silence as disapproval.

BELLINI (CONT'D)
Papal infallibility covers doctrine. It does not extend to appointments.

LAWRENCE
(Beat)
That man is legally a cardinal, Aldo. He has a right to take part in the election.

INT. CASA SANTA MARTA - KITCHEN OFFICE - NIGHT

Benitez stands as LAWRENCE and Bellini walk in.

LAWRENCE
Welcome to the Vatican, Archbishop. I'm Father Lawrence, Dean of the College. This is Father Bellini. I'm sorry you've had to wait. We had to make checks I'm afraid.

Benitez smoothes a lock of dark hair back from his rather boyish face.

BENITEZ
It is I who must apologise for such an unexpected entrance.

BELLINI
(Reluctantly)
Archbishop, forgive me, but I have to say I think you've made a mistake coming here.

BENITEZ
Why is that, Your Eminence?

Bellini looks between the two men - *isn't it obvious?*

BELLINI
I would have thought the position of Christians in Central Asia was perilous enough without you having been made a cardinal and showing yourself in Rome.

BENITEZ
I'm aware of the risks.

BELLINI
But now you're here I don't see how you expect to go back.

BENITEZ
I'll go back. And face the consequences of my faith, like so many others.

Bellini tilts a head, as if to say - *charming but naive.*

BELLINI
Your return will have diplomatic repercussions and therefore will not, *necessarily,* be your decision.

BENITEZ
(Mildly)
Nor yours, Eminence. It will be a decision for the next Pope.

Bellini opens his mouth and closes it again. Lawrence examines the fragile looking man, reevaluating. He's tougher than he looks.

LAWRENCE
Well, the first thing is to find you a room. Where's your luggage?

BENITEZ
I don't have any.

LAWRENCE
None?

BENITEZ
I thought it best to go to the airport empty-handed, to disguise my intentions.

LAWRENCE
(Recovering)
Ray?

O'Malley pops his head in.

LAWRENCE (CONT'D)
His Eminence will require toiletries, some clean clothes, and choir dress of course.
(To Benitez)
Monsignor O'Malley will look after you.

Looking suddenly exhausted, Benitez follows O'Malley out of the office. Lawrence glances at Bellini, a little puzzled by his friend's faint hostility. Bellini shrugs, as if a little puzzled himself.

BELLINI
(Half-apologetic)
It's just so...irregular.

INT. CASA SANTA MARTA - CORRIDOR - NIGHT

Lawrence walks down the corridor to his room and finds Adeyemi approaching from the other end. He raises a hand in greeting. Both stop at the mid-point of the corridor.

LAWRENCE
We're neighbours, Joshua.

ADEYEMI
It seems so.

They stand smiling, slightly awkwardly, key cards in hand.

LAWRENCE
(making conversation)
I thought - a little more work on my homily for tomorrow...

ADEYEMI
Ah, yes of course... I look forward to it.
(Mock conspiratorial)
I understand the trick is to offend no-one.

He chuckles at his own joke.

ADEYEMI (CONT'D)
Well...

They nod to each other and both go into their rooms.

INT. CASA SANTA MARTA - LAWRENCE'S ROOM - NIGHT

Lawrence sits, back to us, hunched over the small desk, staring at the shuttered window in front of him, lost in thought.

From the next room, through the thin walls, he hears the sound of coughing, a toilet flushing...

He stirs, picks up his pen and resumes work on his sermon.

INT. CASA SANTA MARTA - LAWRENCE'S BATHROOM - NIGHT

CLOSE ON LAWRENCE - staring at us.

LAWRENCE
(Italian)
< *Our recent Popes have all been tireless promoters of peace and co-operation at the international level. Let us pray that the future Pope will continue this ceaseless work of charity and love...* >

LAWRENCE
I nostri ultimi Papi sono stati tutti instancabili promotori di pace e cooperazione a livello internazionale. Preghiamo che il futuro Papa continui questa incessante opera di carità e amore...

We realise Lawrence is practicing his sermon in his BATHROOM, before the mirror.

He stops, feels a twinge of contempt for its bland tone.

He puts the sermon aside, examines the cheap little plastic wrapped package of razor, tooth brush and toothpaste, fumbles with it for a moment.

He finally rips it open and its contents fall to the floor. Lawrence sighs, examines his reflection again for a moment.

LAWRENCE (CONT'D)
You're a manager.
(Beat)
Manage.

INT. CASA SANTA MARTA - DINING ROOM - NIGHT

CLOSE ON SISTER AGNES

...a watchful silent presence, as ever. She monitors the nuns as they fan through the...

...LARGE ROOM running down one side of the lobby. White marble floors, tables set for dinner, the din of conversation from the assembled cardinals. It could be a business convention.

Her gaze lands on the Americans seated at one table, talking loudly. Tremblay in the middle, joking and laughing with them.

Lawrence takes a knife and glass and raps it for attention. The room gradually falls silent except for Cardinal KRASINSKI, the arch-conservative Archbishop Emeritus of Chicago who continues speaking loudly until he is hushed by his neighbours, and adjusts his hearing-aid, resulting in an electronic howl that causes them to wince.

Benitez standing alone, apart.

LAWRENCE
Your Eminences, before we eat I should like to introduce a new member of our order, whose existence was not known to any of us until a few hours ago.
(Raising a hand to the stir of surprise)
This is because our brother was made a cardinal by a perfectly legitimate procedure known as creation *in pectore*. The reason why it had to be done this way is known only to God and to the late Holy Father. But I think we can guess well enough as our new brother's ministry is an extremely dangerous one.
(MORE)

LAWRENCE (CONT'D)
It has not been an easy journey for him to join us but now, by the Grace of God a brotherhood of one hundred and seven has become one hundred and eight. Welcome to our order, Vincent Benitez, Cardinal Archbishop of Kabul.

A general sense of mystification from his audience. He begins to applaud and for a painful moment he is the only one clapping. Gradually the others join in.

LAWRENCE (CONT'D)
Would you bless our meal, Eminence?

Benitez looks alarmed at the prospect but nods. The cardinals lower their heads, eyes closed.

BENITEZ
Bless us, O Lord, and these Your gifts which we are about to receive from Your bounty.

Several of the cardinals begin to make the sign of the cross, presuming this is the end.

BENITEZ (CONT'D)
(in Spanish)
Bless too, all those who cannot share this meal. And help us, O Lord, as we eat and drink, to remember the hungry, the thirsty, the sick and the lonely, and those sisters who prepared this food for us. Through Christ Our Lord, Amen.

BENITEZ (CONT'D)
Bendice también a todos aquellos que no pueden compartir esta comida con nosotros. Y, mientras comemos y bebemos, ayúdanos Señor a recordar a los que pasan hambre, a los que están sedientos, a los enfermos y a los que están solos, y a las hermanas que nos han
preparado esta comida. Por *
Cristo Nuestro Señor, Amén.

A rumble of Amens and the Sisters begin to serve the meal. Lawrence leads Benitez over to a table with Asian cardinals then heads on himself towards Bellini.

TEDESCO
(Italian)
< *Dean!* >

TEDESCO
Decano!

With dismay Lawrence finds himself beside the Patriarch of Venice's table. Tedesco indicates an empty seat.

TEDESCO (CONT'D)
(Italian)
< *Take s ome wine.* >

TEDESCO (CONT'D)
Prendete del vino.

Lawrence reluctantly sits and accepts the glass. Tedesco observes him as he continues to eat with gusto.

TEDESCO (CONT'D)
(Italian)
< You look anxious. And we haven't even begun yet. >
(Chewing)
< Our new brother...did I hear correctly? Afghanistan?>

TEDESCO (CONT'D)
Sembrate ansioso. E non abbiamo nemmeno iniziato.
(Chewing)
Our new brother.. ho capito bene? "Afghanistan"?

LAWRENCE
(Italian)
< I did. >

LAWRENCE
Sì.

He looks around the dining room.

LAWRENCE (CONT'D)
(Italian)
< A marvellous testament to the Universal Church, don't you think? So many men of different cultures, races, bound together by their faith in God. >

LAWRENCE (CONT'D)
Una meravigliosa testimonianza della Chiesa universale, non crede? Tanti uomini di culture e razze diverse, legati dalla fede in Dio.

Tedesco grunts in amusement as he eats.

TEDESCO
(Italian)
< Look again. Notice how everyone has gravitated to their fellow countrymen. Italians over here... Spanish speakers there...English there... Divided by language. When we were boys and the Tridentine Mass was still the liturgy of the world - we would all have been speaking Latin. But then your fellow liberals insisted we get rid of that "dead" language. You say "Universal" Church, but we have become a confederation at best. >

TEDESCO
Guardate bene. Notate come *
tutti hanno gravitato intorno ai loro connazionali. Noi italiani di qua... gli spagnoli di là... gli inglesi
di là... 'divided by *
language'. Quando eravamo ragazzi e la Messa tridentina era ancora la liturgia del mondo, avremmo parlato tutti latino. Ma poi i vostri colleghi liberali hanno insistito perché ci liberassimo di quella lingua
"morta". Lei dice "universal *
church", ma semmai siamo *
diventati una confederazione.

LAWRENCE
(in English)
The church i s evolving, Goffredo.

TEDESCO
(in English)
Disintegrating.

Tedesco's fellow traditionalists at the table are staring stonily at Lawrence, as if holding him personally responsible.

TEDESCO (CONT'D)
(Italian)
< Another Holy Father like the last one and our Mother the Church will cease to exist. Without Rome, without the tradition of Rome... >
(changes to English)
... "things fall apart, the centre cannot hold."

TEDESCO (CONT'D)
Un altro Santo Padre come l'ultimo e la nostra Madre Chiesa cesserà di esistere. Senza Roma, senza la tradizione di Roma...
(changes to English)
... "things fall apart, the centre cannot hold."

LAWRENCE
So... what? The next Pope must be Italian?

TEDESCO
(Italian)
< We haven't had an Italian Pope for more than forty years. Can you seriously imagine the alternative? >

TEDESCO
Sono più di quarant'anni che non abbiamo un Papa italiano. Può seriamente immaginare l'alternativa? Abyssus abyssum invocat. *

His gaze slides to the table of African cardinals, Adeyemi in the middle. This is too much.

LAWRENCE
(Italian)
< Excuse me. I must circulate amongst our colleagues. >

LAWRENCE
Scusatemi, devo fare il giro tra i nostri Confratelli.

He stands, bows his head to the circle of hostile faces and walks off.

INT. CASA SANTA MARTA - AULA - NIGHT

Lawrence sits with Bellini and his circle of liberal supporters, having a coffee after their meal.

LAWRENCE
I'll give him this, he clearly has no intention of tempering his views to win votes.

CARDINAL SABBADIN
It was shrewd of him to stay away from Rome until today. One outspoken newspaper interview could have written Tedesco off. Instead, he will do well tomorrow, I think.

LAWRENCE
Define "well."

Sabbadin rocks his head from side to side, appraising.

CARDINAL SABBADIN
I'd say he's worth fifteen votes in the first ballot.

LAWRENCE
And your man?

Bellini looks pained as Sabbadin studies him in the same thoughtful way.

BELLINI
Why do I feel like a cow being priced by the farmer?

CARDINAL SABBADIN
(Ignoring this)
First ballot? Between twenty and twenty-five. But it's tomorrow night that the real work begins. Somehow we have to get him a two-thirds majority.

BELLINI
By real work, you mean - what, exactly?

CARDINAL LANDOLFI
Your Eminence, those who seek the papacy...

BELLINI
(Irritated)
I don't "seek" the papacy. I...

He is interrupted as the door opens and a Sister comes to pick up a tray of empty coffee cups. The men sit in uncomfortable silence until the nun has moved on.

CARDINAL VILLANUEVA
Listen you don't have to do anything, leave it to us. But if they ask us what you stand for...?

BELLINI
Tell them I stand for a common-sense approach to issues such as gays, or divorce. Tell them I stand for never returning to the days of the Latin liturgy, families of ten children because Mamma and Papa know no better.
(MORE)

BELLINI (CONT'D)
It was an ugly, repressive time and I'm glad it's over. Tell them I stand for respecting other faiths, tolerating other views within our own Church. And tell them I believe women should play more of a role within the Curia...

Sabbadin winces, sucks his teeth.

CARDINAL SABBADIN
Let's... let's not mention women.

BELLINI
Brother, I have no intention of concealing my views or pretending to be anything other than I am in order to try and sway any of our number who are undecided. So if you are going to canvas on my behalf, make sure my message is clear... Tell them that I stand for everything *Tedesco* does not.
(Beat)
Now, if you'll excuse me...

He stands up and leaves. Sabbadin sighs, polishes his glasses.

CARDINAL SABBADIN
Rocco, you talk to the Americans. Villanueva, I'll leave the South Americans to you. Gianmarco, you take the Africans. And, obviously, no mention of women.

Lawrence watches Bellini walk away, feeling a stab of pity for him.

LAWRENCE
He doesn't want this. Any of it. You know that don't you?

CARDINAL SABBADIN
Of course. That's why I support him. The men who are dangerous are the ones who actively desire it.

Lawrence ponders on this.

INT. CASA SANTA MARTA - TREMBLAY'S ROOM - NIGHT

Darkness. Silence.

Then a door opens, a switch is flicked and Tremblay's room glares into light. It's a suite, like the Pope's.

TREMBLAY
(Letting Lawrence in)
I'm enjoying the mystery Thomas but I suppose you should tell me what you want to talk about?

Lawrence hesitates, but the sooner he gets this over with the sooner they can put it behind them.

LAWRENCE
Your last meeting with the Holy Father.

TREMBLAY
Uhuh? What about it?

LAWRENCE
I've been told it was difficult. Was it?

TREMBLAY
(Surprised)
Difficult? No? Not that I can recall.

Lawrence hesitates again.

LAWRENCE
I'm sorry to have to ask this, Joe, but... To be specific, I was told that the Holy Father demanded your resignation.

Tremblay looks genuinely shocked.

TREMBLAY
(Beat)
That's absurd. I don't know what... *who* told you?

LAWRENCE
(Beat)
Archbishop Wozniak.

TREMBLAY
(Beat)
Why would he *say* such a thing?

LAWRENCE
So, there isn't *any* truth in the allegation?

TREMBLAY
God, no, of course not! It's absurd. You didn't think...?

LAWRENCE
I had to ask.

TREMBLAY
No, I understand, of course. But, no.
(A sudden thought)
You can ask Monsignor Morales. He was *at* the meeting.

LAWRENCE
I would but at the moment we happen to be sequestered.

Tremblay shakes his head, walks to the coffee machine.

LAWRENCE (CONT'D)
Can you think of any reason why Archbishop Wozniak would circulate such a story?

TREMBLAY
I can't. I really...coffee?
(Lawrence shakes his head)
I'm quite... I'm shocked.
He told you this himself?

Lawrence nods. Tremblay shakes his head again, raises a baffled hand. He collects his coffee, stares at it.

TREMBLAY (CONT'D)
Do you think...?

He hesitates, embarrassed.

LAWRENCE
What?

Tremblay looks up at him, a little guiltily.

TREMBLAY
The drinking? (Beat) I don't like to bring it up, but we both know his drinking has been getting heavier and perhaps it's affecting his judgement, his mind even? I know my name has been mentioned as a future Pope and if the Archbishop does not approve of the idea then perhaps...

He waves a hand again, embarrassed.

TREMBLAY (CONT'D)
I don't know. I'm just trying to make sense of... and I know the poor man was shattered by the Holy Father's death.

He finishes his espresso. Lawrence is desperate for this to be over.

LAWRENCE
Yes. Indeed. Again, Joe, my apologies for...

TREMBLAY
No, not at all. I quite understand.

They head for the door. Then to his own surprise, Lawrence says...

LAWRENCE
What *did* you discuss with the Holy Father in that final meeting?

Tremblay blinks. When he answers his manner is a little cooler - as if the insult of the accusation has just caught up with him.

TREMBLAY
Forgive me, but it was a private conversation, Thomas. And very precious. The last words I exchanged with the Holy Father.

Beat. Then Lawrence inclines his head.

LAWRENCE
I quite understand.

Tremblay opens the door in silence, waits for Lawrence to step out the room then switches off the brilliant lights, closes the door plunging us into darkness.

We HOLD in the black...

OMITTED

INT. CASA SANTA MARTA - LAWRENCE'S ROOM - NIGHT

Lawrence wakes suddenly. From the next room comes the sound of stentorian snoring. He tries to screen it out. But sleep seems impossible now. He sits up in bed.

INT. CASA SANTA MARTA - GYM - NIGHT

Lawrence walks on the treadmill, the only figure in the large room. He stares at his reflection in the mirrored wall as he speed walks, listening to the hypnotic *thrum, thrum* of the treadmill.

TITLE CARD: **FIRST DAY OF CONCLAVE**

EXT. CASA SANTA MARTA - COURTYARD - MORNING

HIGH ANGLE - from the top of the balcony. The courtyard below is a sea of red: cardinals robed for the coming service.

Lawrence stands staring down at them, an air of trepidation behind the eyes. Below a single nun in blue is lost among the red.

FATHER HAAS (O.S.)
Your Eminence?

Behind him Father Haas has appeared in the hall. Lawrence blinks out of his thoughts.

INT. CASA SANTA MARTA - SIDE ROOM - MORNING

Haas is robing Lawrence, fussing around like a tailor, adjusting the heavy red chasuble. He places the tall, white mitre on Lawrence's head, stands back to survey its angle critically. He hands Lawrence the crozier - a golden Shepherd's crook.

FATHER HAAS
How does it feel, Your Eminence?

LAWRENCE
Good. Thank you.

We hear the chanting of the *Gospel of St John...*

INT. "ROOM OF CARDINALS" - MORNING

A bare space. Lawrence looks out at the rows of the congregation that have been crammed into the room: the red of the cardinals, purple of the Bishops, white of the Priests... They sit and stand in front of him.

Lawrence sits, clutching the sermon in his lap, hiding the turmoil going on inside him. His gaze flits across the ranks of cardinals, finding the main contenders: Adeyemi, Bellini, Tremblay and finally Tedesco. Haas appears in front of him and removes the mitre, catches something in the Dean's expression as he does so.

FATHER HAAS
(Concerned, softly)
Are you well, Eminence?

LAWRENCE
I'm fine.

The choir comes to an end.

ON THE MICROPHONE - as Lawrence steps in front of it. For a moment he stares out over the room of faces. He stares down at the pages of homily. The moment hangs until there's a faint stirring of unease. Finally...

LAWRENCE (CONT'D)
(Reading, Italian)
< Dear Brothers in Christ, at this moment of great uncertainty in the history of the Holy Church we must think first of the late Holy Father whose brilliant pontificate was a gift from God. >

LAWRENCE (CONT'D)
Cari fratelli in Cristo, in questo momento di grande incertezza nella storia della Santa Chiesa dobbiamo pensare innanzitutto al defunto Santo Padre, il cui brillante pontificato è stato un dono di Dio.

A murmur of approval from the congregation.

LAWRENCE (CONT'D)
< Now we must ask our Lord to send us a new Holy Father through the pastoral solicitude of the cardinal fathers and we must pray to God for that loving assistance and ask Him to guide us to the right choice.>

LAWRENCE (CONT'D)
Ora dobbiamo chiedere a nostro Signore di mandarci un nuovo Santo Padre attraverso la sollecitudine pastorale dei padri cardinali e dobbiamo pregare Dio per questa amorevole assistenza e chiedere la sua guida nel compiere la scelta giusta.

He looks out at his audience, his gaze once more falling on Tedesco watching him with a faint complacent smile.

He turns the page, scans the text, and the next page... platitudes, platitudes...

Suddenly he puts the sermon aside. For the first time in days he feels calm.

LAWRENCE (CONT'D)
(In English)
But you all know that.

There is some surprised laughter.

LAWRENCE (CONT'D)
Let me speak from the heart for the moment.

Now there's a definite stirring of alarm amongst the cardinals.

LAWRENCE (CONT'D)
St Paul said "Be subject to one another out of reverence for Christ." To work together, and grow together, we must be tolerant.

The room is entirely still now...

INTERCUT WITH:

INT. "ROOM OF CARDINALS" ANTECHAMBER - MORNING

... whilst right outside the door SISTER AGNES and a few of her nuns are silently listening to Lawrence's speech.

LAWRENCE
St Paul said that God's gift to the Church is its variety. It is this variety, this *diversity* of people and views that gives our Church its strength. In the course of a long life in the service of our Mother the Church, let me tell you that there is one sin I have come to fear above all others. Certainty. Certainty is the great enemy of unity. Certainty is the deadly enemy of tolerance. Even Christ was not certain at the end.

Lawrence switches into Italian.

LAWRENCE (CONT'D)
"Dio mio, Dio mio, perché mi hai abbandonato?"

LAWRENCE (CONT'D)
(back to English)
"My God, my God, why have you forsaken me?" He cried out in His agony at the ninth hour on the cross. Our faith is a living thing precisely *because* it walks hand in hand with doubt. If there was only certainty, and if there was no doubt, there would be no mystery, and therefore no need for faith. Let us pray that God will grant us a Pope who doubts. Let Him grant us a Pope who sins and asks for forgiveness. And carries on.

He looks out over the cardinals and sees they are unified by a single emotion. Shock.

EXT. CASA SANTA MARTA - COURTYARD - DAY

Lawrence is led by Haas and some ASSISTANTS through the courtyard, crowded with cardinals. Lawrence feels their eyes upon him.

INT. CASA SANTA MARTA - SIDE ROOM - DAY

Lawrence stands being disrobed by Haas and the Assistants. None of the younger men can look Lawrence in the face. O'Malley arrives holding the discarded sermon.

MONSIGNOR O'MALLEY
(Awkward)
Dean, your homily... I'm not entirely clear whether or not it should be placed in the Vatican archive or not? As it was not the homily you... actually... delivered?

LAWRENCE
I'm not sure either.

Lawrence examines the usually ebullient Irishman and realises even he is avoiding his gaze.

LAWRENCE (CONT'D)
Was it that bad, Ray?

MONSIGNOR O'MALLEY
(Hurriedly)
Not at all, Your Eminence. It has caused quite a stir. I don't think anyone expected you to... to...

LAWRENCE
(Smiling)
Say something interesting?

Haas lifts the chasuble over his head, and LAWRENCE rotates his stiff neck, relieved to be free of the weight.

LAWRENCE (CONT'D)
(As Haas leaves)
Thank you, Father.

MONSIGNOR O'MALLEY
I'll have a transcript made of the text from the tape, Eminence. If there's nothing else...

Lawrence hesitates, as O'Malley turns to go. Then...

LAWRENCE
I need you to do something for me. Monsignor Morales. I'm sure he's still in Rome. Could you try and see him? Use my authority.

MONSIGNOR O'MALLEY
(Surprised)
Today? I...I could try, your Eminence?

LAWRENCE
I need to know what happened in the final meeting between the Holy Father and Cardinal Tremblay.

MONSIGNOR O'MALLEY
What...*happened?*

Lawrence takes a deep breath, and...

LAWRENCE
Specifically, did anything occur that might render Cardinal Tremblay unfit to assume the papacy?

O'Malley gapes at him, recovers himself.

MONSIGNOR O'MALLEY
Of course, Eminence.

LAWRENCE
Bless you.

INT. CASA SANTA MARTA - LOBBY - DAY

Lawrence is heading for the lift when...

TEDESCO (O.S.)
(Booming, Italian)
< *Well, Dean...* >

TEDESCO (O.S.)
(tonante)
Beh, Decano...

Lawrence turns to find Tedesco advancing on him, drawing the attention of the crowded lobby.

TEDESCO (CONT'D)
(Italian)
< St Paul as an Apostle of Doubt. I've never heard that one before! >

TEDESCO (CONT'D)
San Paolo come apostolo del dubbio. Non l'avevo mai sentita prima!

Lawrence continues to the lift, determined to avoid a public argument.

TEDESCO (CONT'D)
< Wasn't it St Paul who said, "If the trumpet shall give an uncertain note, who will prepare himself for battle?">

TEDESCO (CONT'D)
Non è stato forse San Paolo a dire: "E se la tromba emette un suono confuso, chi si preparerà alla battaglia?"

Lawrence presses for the lift and the doors glide open.

LAWRENCE
(in Latin)
Perhaps it would have been more palatable for you in Latin, Eminence?

He steps into the lift before Tedesco can reply.

INT. CASA SANTA MARTA - LOBBY LIFT - DAY

Lawrence, a little pleased with his retort, is about to press the button for his floor when he suddenly pats his pockets. He closes his eyes.

INT. CASA SANTA MARTA - LOBBY - DAY

Lawrence emerges from the lift again, to the surprise of Tedesco and the other cardinals. Aware he's just ruined his exit, he walks back to the RECEPTION DESK, trying to look unconcerned.

LAWRENCE
I'm sorry, I forgot my key.

SISTER AGNES examines him sternly from behind the desk.

SISTER AGNES
I hope you take better care of the Keys of St Peter than you do of the keys to your room.

She reaches under the counter and hands him a KEY CARD.

SISTER AGNES (CONT'D)
That's my pass key. If you could remember to return it.

Lawrence nods, feeling like a scolded child. Sister Agnes walks into the back office. Lawrence turns to find Bellini standing beside him. His friend gives an awful smile.

BELLINI
(Quietly)
Well, I'm puzzled. You tell me you wanted to resign and then you step out of the shadows like this?

It takes Lawrence a moment to realise there is anger in Bellini's voice.

BELLINI (CONT'D)
Now - who knows how things may turn out?

He's gone before Lawrence can think of a reply.

EXT. CASA SANTA MARTA - PARKING - DAY

The cardinals are boarding a fleet of white minibuses as it begins to rain.

MONSIGNOR O'MALLEY
(Directing the boarding)
Cardinal Gambino... Cardinal Dell'Acqua...

Lawrence waits to board, still thinking of Bellini's words. We hear an organ playing, a choir singing *Veni Creator Spiritus...*

I/E. MINIBUS - DAY

As the music continues we find Lawrence sitting alone, biretta on his lap, staring out the rain-smeared windows to the security men patrolling the Vatican grounds beyond. The cardinals all around him are silent, the mood on the bus is sombre, the moment of responsibility has come.

EXT. CORTILE DEL MARESCIALLO - DAY

A narrow strip of grey sky above the parked buses. Security forces linger about, smoking and chatting. The bus driver eats a sandwich.

INT. SCALA REGIA - DAY

A security guard scrolls through his phone, standing on the marble staircase. We hear the cardinals taking their oath.

JUNIOR CARDINAL-DEACON GUERRINI (O.S.)
(In Latin)
< *...I Antonio Cardinal Guerrini do so promise, pledge and swear, so help me God and these Holy Gospels which I touch with my hand.* >

JUNIOR CARDINAL-DEACON GUERRINI (O.S.)
...Et ego Antonius Cardinalis Guerrini spondeo, voveo ac iuro, Sic me Deus adiuvet et haec Sancta Dei Evangelia, quae manu mea tango.

INT. SISTINE CHAPEL - DAY

The last of the cardinals stand taking the oath. The others have now taken their seats at the rows of desks filling the room.

CARDINAL BROTZKUS
(In Latin)
< *...I Romuald Cardinal Brotzkus do so promise, pledge and swear...* >

CARDINAL BROTZKUS
...Et ego Romualdus Cardinalis Brotzkus spondeo, voveo ac iuro...

Lawrence finds himself staring up at Michelangelo's *The Last Judgement*. One of the Damned clutches a hand to his face as demons drag him down...

CARDINAL BROTZKUS (CONT'D)
< *So help me God and these Holy Gospels which I touch with my hand.* >

CARDINAL BROTZKUS (CONT'D)
Sic me Deus adiuvet et haec Sancta Dei Evangelia, quae manu mea tango.

CARDINAL NAKITANDA
Et ego Irumbus Cardinalis Nakitanda spondeo, voveo ac iuro, sic me Deus adiuvet et haec Sancta Dei Evangelia, quae manu mea tango.

Lawrence blinks as Mandorff steps up to the microphone that has been placed before the west wall of the chamber.

ARCHBISHOP MANDORFF
Extra omnes.

The television lights are switched off plunging the chamber into relative gloom. Mandorff makes his way to the vestibule as priests, officials, choristers, security men, cameramen, photographer and the commandant of the Swiss Guard leave the chapel. The three scrutineers, CARDINALS LUKSA, MERCURIO and LOMBARDI, take their place at a table in front of the altar.

Lawrence catches Adeyemi's eye. Cardinal Tedesco glances at Bellini who looks at Tremblay across from him.

In the vestibule Mandorff passes through the huge doors...

INT. OUTSIDE SISTINE CHAPEL - DAY

...to close them after him.

INT. SISTINE CHAPEL - DAY

We hear the sound of a key turning. The great bell of St Peter's begins tolling five o'clock.

<u>The Conclave has begun</u>.

LAWRENCE walks to the microphone.

LAWRENCE

< Cardinal brothers, we will now proceed to the first ballot. >

(Holding up a ballot paper)

< You will find in front of you your ballot paper. On the top half is written... >

(Glancing ironically at Tedesco)

< Eligo in Summum Pontificem. "I elect as Supreme Pontiff". Beneath this you must write the name of your chosen candidate. Please make sure your hand-writing is legible.>

LAWRENCE

Fratelli Cardinali, procederà ora al primo scrutinio.

(Holding up a paper ballot)

Troverete davanti a voi la vostra scheda elettorale. Sulla metà superiore è scritto...

(Glancing Ironically at Tedesco)

Eligo in Summum Pontificem. "Eleggo Sommo Pontefice". Sotto di essa dovete scrivere il nome del candidato che avete scelto. Assicuratevi che la vostra calligrafia sia leggibile.

Lawrence returns to his seat and picks up his own ballot paper. He shields the paper with his arm and writes BELLINI, folds it and walks back to the altar. He holds it above his head.

LAWRENCE (CONT'D)

(In Latin)

< I call as my witness Christ the Lord who will be my judge, that my vote is given to the one who before God I think should be elected. >

LAWRENCE (CONT'D)

Testor Christum Dominum, qui me iudicaturus est, me eum eligere, quem secundum Deum iudico eligi debere.

Under the gaze of the three cardinals he places his ballot in the large urn on the altar.

He returns to his seat, his eyes straying to where Bellini sits, apparently sunk in meditation. One by one the cardinals begin to rise and vote, ballots held above their heads...

INT. SISTINE CHAPEL - DAY / LATER

The three Scrutineers sit at the table in front of the altar, counting the votes from the urn. Luksa unfolds a ballot, notes the name, passes it to Lombardi who also records the result and passes it to Mercurio who pierces the vote through the word elect and threads it onto a length of scarlet silk cord.

CARDINAL LOMBARDI
(Italian)
< *The first vote is cast for Cardinal Tedesco.* >

CARDINAL LOMBARDI
Il primo voto è per il Cardinale Tedesco.

Lawrence doesn't react, just makes a tick next to Tedesco's name on his list of cardinals. Lombardi reads the next ballot.

CARDINAL LOMBARDI (CONT'D)
(Italian)
< *The second vote is cast for Cardinal Tedesco.* >

CARDINAL LOMBARDI (CONT'D)
Il secondo voto è per il Cardinale Tedesco.

Again. Lombardi records the next ballot.

CARDINAL LOMBARDI (CONT'D)
(Italian)
Cardinal Tremblay.

CARDINAL LOMBARDI (CONT'D)
Cardinale Tremblay.

Lawrence ticks the name...

CARDINAL LOMBARDI (CONT'D)
(Reading the next ballot)
< *Cardinal Tremblay.* >

CARDINAL LOMBARDI (CONT'D)
(Reading the next ballot)
Cardinale Tremblay.

...and again...

CARDINAL LOMBARDI (CONT'D)
< *Cardinal Lawrence.* >

CARDINAL LOMBARDI (CONT'D)
Cardinale Lawrence.

Lawrence looks up, startled. He finds Bellini watching him.

CARDINAL LOMBARDI (CONT'D)
< *Cardinal Bellini.* >

CARDINAL LOMBARDI (CONT'D)
Cardinale Bellini.

Lawrence focuses on his list again, hurriedly ticking the names...

INT. SISTINE CHAPEL - DAY / LATER

CLOSE on the URN - now almost empty of ballots. Luksa's hand reaches in.

Lawrence is hurriedly adding up the votes in pencil beside his list.

CARDINAL LOMBARDI
< *Cardinal Bellini.* >
(Italian, Receiving the next ballot)
< *Cardinal Tremblay.* >
(Beat)
< *Cardinal Adeyemi.* >

CARDINAL LOMBARDI
Cardinale Bellini.
(Italian, Receiving the next ballot)
Cardinale Tremblay.
(Beat)
Cardinale Adeyemi.

Lawrence scribbles away...

CARDINAL LOMBARDI (CONT'D)
< *And finally... Cardinal Benitez.* >

CARDINAL LOMBARDI (CONT'D)
E infine... Cardinale Benítez.

Again, Lawrence looks up in surprise. Benitez himself has raised his head in shock. Whispered conversations break out around the chamber. The three Scrutineers confer briefly then Lombardi leans into the microphone again.

CARDINAL LOMBARDI (CONT'D)
(Italian)
< *The results of the first ballot are... Cardinal Adeyemi, twenty-one votes. Cardinal Tedesco, eighteen votes. Cardinal Bellini, seventeen votes. Cardinal Tremblay, sixteen votes. Cardinal Lawrence, five votes...* >

CARDINAL LOMBARDI (CONT'D)
I risultati del primo scrutinio sono i seguenti: Cardinale Adeyemi, ventuno voti. Cardinale Tedesco, diciotto voti. Cardinale Bellini, diciassette voti. Cardinale Tremblay, sedici voti. Cardinale Lawrence, cinque voti...

Lawrence flinches, dismayed at this.

CARDINAL LOMBARDI (CONT'D)
< *Other cardinals assigned a single vote, thirty-one votes.* >

CARDINAL LOMBARDI (CONT'D)
Altri cardinali che hanno ricevuto un solo voto, trentuno voti.

The hum of conversation grows louder as Lawrence stands and walks to the microphone.

LAWRENCE
(Raising his voice over the hubbub)
< *My brother cardinals... my brother cardinals, that concludes the first ballot. No candidate having achieved the necessary majority of seventy-two votes, we shall adjourn for the evening and resume voting in the morning. I now invite the Junior Cardinal-Deacon to ask for us to be released.* >

LAWRENCE
(Raising his voice above the hubbub)
Fratelli cardinali... fratelli cardinali, con questo si conclude il primo scrutinio. Poiché nessun candidato ha ottenuto la maggioranza necessaria di settantadue voti, per la serata la seduta è aggiornata e riprenderemo le votazioni domattina. Ora invito l'ultimo cardinale diacono a dire che ci vengano ad aprire.

His gaze flits to Bellini, who sits, staring into nothing. Guerrini walks to the back of the chapel and knocks on the doors.

JUNIOR CARDINAL-DEACON GUERRINI
Aprite le porte! Aprite le porte!

INT. OUTSIDE SISTINE CHAPEL - DAY

Archbishop Mandorff waits outside the Sistine Chapel. He now unlocks the doors and they begin to swing open...

INT. SISTINE CHAPEL - VESTIBULE - LATE AFTERNOON

Monsignor O'Malley squats by the stove, their chimneys rising to a window high above. He bundles inside the threaded ballot papers. He ignites them with a fire-lighter, closes the door as they begin to blaze. He turns to the second stove and presses a switch.

INT. INSIDE THE STOVE - LATE AFTERNOON

INSIDE THE STOVE - the canister of potassium perchlorate, anthracene and sulphur activates with a *whoosh*...

EXT. SISTINE CHAPEL - LATE AFTERNOON

The temporary metal chimney jutting out above the roof of the chapel begins to gush jet-black smoke, illuminated by a search-light. The smoke streams up to the winter sky and the waiting world. A dull roar swells and fades. It takes us a moment to realise it's the response of the vast crowd gathered outside.

INT. EMPTY ROOMS - LATE AFTERNOON

As the dull roar continues to resound from outside rooms inside the Vatican lie still and empty in the late afternoon light. The canary listens in his cage.

INT. SALA REGIA - LATE AFTERNOON

Lawrence and O'Malley hurry through the hall.

MONSIGNOR O'MALLEY

The media have noticed the presence of a cardinal who doesn't appear on the official lists, Dean. The press office have been receiving requests for information, so I've taken the liberty of putting together a draft statement. I've also put together some biographical details for you.

(Glancing through some sheets of paper)

Ministries in Veracruz, the Congo, established a hospital for female victims of the genocidal sexual violence during the first and second wars. Then Baghdad. And finally the Mission in Kabul. There was some question of his resigning on health grounds, but apparently the Holy Father convinced him to continue.

(Handing the sheets to Lawrence)

He's certainly served his ministry in some terrible places.

LAWRENCE

(Absently)

On health grounds? Look into that will you Ray? Kind of thing the press like to get hold of.

Lawrence glances back at the SECURITY MAN who follows them at a discrete distance.

LAWRENCE (CONT'D)

(Quietly)

And the other matter...?

INT. SCALA REGIA - LATE AFTERNOON

The two men descend the stairs, dwarfed by the vast sweep of white marble. Another SECURITY MAN waits below them.

MONSIGNOR O'MALLEY
I spoke to Monsignor Morales. He was emphatic that he knows of no reason why Cardinal Tremblay should not be Pope.

Lawrence nods, wonders why he does not feel any relief.

LAWRENCE
Thank you.

They pass the SECURITY GUARD who turns and whispers into his sleeve. When they are safely past, O'Malley hesitates. Then...

MONSIGNOR O'MALLEY
(Low)
However, will you forgive me if I say that I did not entirely believe the good monsignor?

Lawrence stares at him as they walk on.

MONSIGNOR O'MALLEY (CONT'D)
He was just... so *emphatic?* My Spanish is quite poor and I may have... *accidentally*... given him the impression that you had seen a document that contradicted that? And he said *you weren't to worry about that.* His exact words were - *"El informe ha sido retirado."*

LAWRENCE
A "report?" A report on what? Withdrawn when?

MONSIGNOR O'MALLEY
That I couldn't say, Eminence.

They walk on towards the *Cortile del Maresciallo* and the waiting minibuses.

I/E. MINIBUS - LATE AFTERNOON

Lawrence is last on the bus and the only seat still available is at the front, near Sabbadin.

Reluctantly Lawrence sits down across the aisle from him. For a moment the two sit in silence, Sabbadin staring out of the window. Then...

CARDINAL SABBADIN
(Sourly)
Third place. Not what we had hoped.
(Beat)
Your sermon didn't exactly help us. And your five votes... with the greatest respect Thomas, you have far too little support to emerge as a serious candidate. There hasn't been an English Pope for a thousand years.

LAWRENCE
(Without looking at him)
My position is an embarrassment to me. If I find out who my supporters are I'll plead with them to vote for someone else. And I'll tell them I'll be voting for Bellini.

Sabbadin nods, mollified.

CARDINAL SABBADIN
Alright, that's five votes coming to us, which takes us to twenty-two. All the candidates who received one vote today will fall away. That leaves thirty-one votes available. We simply have to pick up most of them.

Uncomfortable, Lawrence glances at the driver's face in the rear-view mirror, trying to gauge if he has been listening.

INT. CASA SANTA MARTA - DINING ROOM - NIGHT

The cardinals stand around in cliques, sipping wine before the evening meal. Adeyemi, as the front runner, seems to have gathered the largest crowd.

Alone, Lawrence is watching Benitez talking to the cardinals from Asia and Oceania. Cardinal Mendoza arrives beside him, follows his gaze.

CARDINAL MENDOZA
(Of Benitez)
An interesting man. I am very pleased to hear of his elevation.

LAWRENCE
You know him?

CARDINAL MENDOZA
Of him. I was with the Mission in Iraq, after his time, and people still spoke of him there and the work he had done.

TEDESCO (O.S.)
(in English)
So...our dark horse.

Lawrence sighs, turns to find Tedesco and Tremblay beside him, also surveying the room.

LAWRENCE
Don't be absurd. I will do all in my power to withdraw my name from the second vote.

TEDESCO
(English)
Why?

LAWRENCE
Because I don't wish to compromise my neutrality as Dean.

TEDESCO
(English)
Too late.

Tedesco chuckles, continuing in Italian.

TEDESCO (CONT'D)
< Ah, don't worry about it. As far as I'm concerned, I want you to continue as a candidate. You're splitting the liberal vote. >

TEDESCO (CONT'D)
Ah, non preoccupatevi. Per quanto mi riguarda, voglio che restiate in lizza. Grazie a voi il voto dei liberali è diviso.

He pats Lawrence's shoulder and walks off.

LAWRENCE
If anyone brings up my name please tell them of my intentions. All I want to do is serve the Conclave. I can't do that if I'm seen as a contender myself.

Tremblay smiles, nods.

TREMBLAY
Alright.

He gives a short laugh.

TREMBLAY (CONT'D)
Of course, a more Machiavellian mind might say it will make you look like a paragon of virtue.

He laughs again, as if at the absurdity of the suggestion.

LAWRENCE
(Cool)
Well, I shall leave you to handle it as you see fit.

He walks away.

EXT. APOSTOLIC PALACE - PORTONE DI BRONZO - NIGHT

Lawrence and O'Malley walk towards the vast bronze entrance to the palace, past saluting Swiss Guards.

INT. APOSTOLIC PALACE - STAIRCASE - NIGHT

The two walk in silence up the deserted staircase of what would traditionally be the Papal Apartments.

INT. APOSTOLIC PALACE - SALA - NIGHT

They cross a big room and walk into...

INT. PAPAL SECRETARY'S OFFICE - NIGHT

Lawrence stands at a filing cabinet, looking through the folders of documents inside. He checks the final folder, closes the drawer, unsure whether he feels relieved or disappointed. O'Malley watches. A beat.

MONSIGNOR O'MALLEY
(Tentatively)
I could try and speak to Monsignor Morales again? See if I could find out any more?

LAWRENCE
No, no...
(Gesturing to the room, them)
This is all so... unseemly.
(MORE)

LAWRENCE (CONT'D)
If this report ever existed, then I think we can rest assured that it has indeed been withdrawn. We have done all that could be expected of us.

He locks the filing cabinet.

EXT. VATICAN GROUNDS - FOUNTAIN - NIGHT

The two are walking back towards the Casa Santa Marta. Lawrence spots Benitez standing by a FOUNTAIN staring into the water.

LAWRENCE
You go on, Ray.

He walks down a flight of stairs to approach Benitez who is gazing into a pool with swimming TURTLES.

LAWRENCE (CONT'D)
The Holy Father's turtles. He was very fond of them. A gift from Angola.

Benitez looks up with delight.

BENITEZ
I thought for a moment I was imagining them... Where I come from, they are considered very special animals. They symbolise healing and transformation.

LAWRENCE
Well, here they keep escaping and being run over. We should go back - the evening curfew.

EXT. VATICAN GROUNDS - NIGHT

Lawrence and Benitez walk back towards the Casa.

LAWRENCE
How are you bearing up? Your health?

Benitez seems to tense a little at the question.

BENITEZ
My health is excellent, thank you.

LAWRENCE
Oh, I only meant have you recovered from your journey?

BENITEZ
I have indeed.

LAWRENCE
Good. And I noticed in the Sistine that you found someone to vote for?

BENITEZ
(A shy smile)
Yes. I voted for you.
(Off his stricken expression)
Forgive me! Am I not supposed to say?

LAWRENCE
No, it's not... I'm honoured, but...My dear Vincent - may I call you Vincent? - I'm not a serious candidate. My vocation lies in a different...

He struggles to think of a suitable term, then finds himself, to his own surprise, continuing...

LAWRENCE (CONT'D)
After the conclave, I hope to resign as Dean and to leave Rome altogether. So, you see, I...

BENITEZ
Why?

Lawrence is wrong-footed.

LAWRENCE
I have been experiencing some... *difficulties*...

BENITEZ
With your faith?

LAWRENCE
Prayer. I...

He trails off, embarrassed.

BENITEZ
(Understanding)
"I cry out to You, God but You do not answer."

Lawrence shifts uncomfortably - *why did he tell him?*

LAWRENCE
I only mention it to illustrate my point that I am in no way worthy to be Pope.

BENITEZ
Any man who is truly worthy must consider himself unworthy. Isn't that the point you were making in your homily? That without doubt there can be no faith? It resonated with my own experience. In my ministry I have witnessed scenes which would make any man skeptical of God's mercy.

LAWRENCE
(Trying again)
You received a vote yourself didn't you?

BENITEZ
I did. It was absurd.

LAWRENCE
Then imagine how you would feel if I insisted on voting for you and by some miracle you won.

BENITEZ
(Solemnly)
It would be a disaster for the Church.

LAWRENCE
That is how it would be if I became Pope. Think about what I'm asking.

He squeezes his shoulder again and they walk on.

INT. CASA SANTA MARTA - PAPAL CORRIDOR - NIGHT

Lawrence walks along the corridor. He slows as he sees the entrance to the Papal suite, still criss-crossed with ribbons.

On tables on either side of the door, dozens of votive candles flicker. Bellini stands before them, looking lost in thought. Lawrence approaches.

LAWRENCE
Aldo, I feel wretched that my meagre tally may have come at your expense.

He waits for his friend to look at him but Bellini continues to stare at the door. Then...

BELLINI
I had no idea you were so ambitious.

LAWRENCE
(Stung)
That's a ridiculous thing to say.

Bellini turns to him.

BELLINI
Is it...? I thought we had your support. If we liberals are not united then Tedesco will become Pope! You don't know how bad it became, Thomas. The way he and his circle attacked the Holy Father towards the end? The *smears,* the *leaks* to the press. It was *savage...* He fought him every day of his pontificate and now that he's dead he wants to destroy his life's work. If Tedesco wins he will undo sixty years of progress!

Lawrence feels his own temper rising.

LAWRENCE
You talk as if you were the only alternative, Aldo. Adeyemi has the wind behind him...

BELLINI
Adeyemi? A man who believes homosexuals should be sent to prison in this world and hell in the next? Adeyemi isn't the answer to anything and you know it! If you want to defeat...

LAWRENCE
"Defeat?" This is a *Conclave,* Aldo.
You talk as if it's a war.

BELLINI
Because it *is* a war! And you have
to commit to a side! Save your
famous doubts for your prayers!

This knocks the wind out of Lawrence. Neither can quite believe that they're talking to each other like this. Lawrence tries again, quietly, urgently...

LAWRENCE
For God's sake, you cannot
seriously believe I have the
slightest desire to become Pope?

BELLINI
(Dismissing this
contemptuously)
Oh, every cardinal has that desire!
Every cardinal, deep down inside,
has already chosen the name by
which he would like his papacy to
be known!

LAWRENCE
Well, *I* haven't!

BELLINI
Deny it if you like. But search
your heart and *then* tell me it
isn't so.

He walks away leaving a distressed Lawrence staring after him.

INT. CASA SANTA MARTA - LAWRENCE'S ROOM - NIGHT

Lawrence kneels by his bed, in prayer. <u>His eyes stray to the bed itself, anonymous and bland, the padded headboard, a faint echo of a similar moment...</u>

But before he can locate the memory his exhaustion overcomes him. His eyelids flutter, close and slowly he begins to sink forward into sleep...

INT. PAPAL BEDROOM - NIGHT

A DREAM IMAGE

Lawrence straightens, still kneeling by a bed. The LATE POPE lies before him, just as at the opening of the film.

But now his eyes are open and he stares at Lawrence. A charged moment. Something vital is about to be said. Lawrence leans in a little.

The Pope opens his mouth to speak and...

INT. CASA SANTA MARTA - LAWRENCE'S ROOM - NIGHT

... Lawrence wakes in the darkness, hears a muffled conversation, hushed and urgent. A man's baritone. Then, in reply... a woman's voice.

Lawrence reaches out a fumbling hand and switches on the light. Gingerly he straightens up from where he had fallen asleep, slumped over the bed, his joints in agony. He wonders if he dreamed the voice. He checks the clock: 2.55am. Silence. Then he hears it again - a woman's voice, raised, accusatory, Adeyemi's low reply. He pushes against the bed, standing slowly, the un-oiled springs squeak loudly.

He tiptoes across the room and listens at the wall but the voices have fallen silent. After a moment he hears the low rumble of Adeyemi's voice again, followed by the click of a door closing.

He hurries to his own door and opens it...

INT. CASA SANTA MARTA - CORRIDOR - NIGHT

Lawrence peers out into the corridor, just in time to see a flash of the blue uniform as it disappears around the corner.

He stands undecided for a moment, then quietly closes the door and...

INT. CASA SANTA MARTA - LAWRENCE'S ROOM - NIGHT

... sits on his bed, mind whirring.

TITLE CARD: SECOND DAY OF CONCLAVE

EXT. CASA SANTA MARTA - COURTYARD - MORNING

The sea of cardinals mill around the courtyard, ready for the second day of the Conclave. Lawrence, bleary-eyed from his broken night, sees O'Malley approach.

MONSIGNOR O'MALLEY
Good morning, Your Eminence. Did you sleep well?

LAWRENCE
Perfectly, thank you.

MONSIGNOR O'MALLEY
The buses are ready.

Lawrence notices Bellini in the throng, watching him.

LAWRENCE
I think I'll walk.

EXT. VATICAN GARDENS - MORNING

Lawrence walks, aware of the inevitable SECURITY MAN trailing him and the crackle of his walkie-talkie. From the sky above comes the drone of circling helicopters. A gust of wind almost takes Lawrence's zucchetto.

LAWRENCE
(Under his breath)
Oh, do go *away*.

Moments later a figure appears at his side - Adeyemi.

ADEYEMI
Good morning, Dean.

LAWRENCE
Joshua.

They walk in uncomfortable silence for a moment.

ADEYEMI
I want you to know that I very much agreed with your homily yesterday.

Lawrence looks at him in surprise.

ADEYEMI (CONT'D)
We are all tested in our faith, Dean. We all lapse. But the Christian faith is, above all, a message of forgiveness.

LAWRENCE
And tolerance.

ADEYEMI
Exactly. Tolerance. I trust that when this election is over, your moderating voice will be heard in the very highest counsels of the Church. It certainly will be if I have anything to do with it. *The very highest counsels*.

CARDINAL NAKITANDA (O.S.)
Joshua!

ADEYEMI
Excuse me, Dean.

He falls back to talk to two of the African cardinals walking behind them. Lawrence walks on, wondering if Adeyemi has just offered him the position of Secretary of State as a bribe.

INT. SISTINE CHAPEL - MORNING

Pencils scratch the names of cardinals on ballot papers...

Elderly cardinals labour down the aisle, ballots held aloft in shaking hands...

Ballot papers are dropped into the urn...

A needle pierces a ballot paper with scarlet thread...

Cardinal Lombardi leans into the microphone.

CARDINAL LOMBARDI
(Italian)
< The results of the second ballot are... Cardinal Adeyemi: thirty-four votes. Cardinal Tedesco: twenty-five votes. Cardinal Bellini: eighteen votes. Cardinal Tremblay: sixteen votes. Cardinal Lawrence: nine votes... >

CARDINAL LOMBARDI
I risultati del secondo scrutinio sono i seguenti. Cardinale Adeyemi: trentaquattro voti. Cardinale Tedesco: venticinque voti. Cardinale Bellini: diciotto voti. Cardinale Tremblay: sedici voti. Cardinale Lawrence: nove voti...

Lawrence barely has time to register this increase in his tally before...

CARDINAL LOMBARDI (CONT'D)
< Cardinal Benitez: two votes. Other cardinals assigned a single vote: four votes. >

CARDINAL LOMBARDI (CONT'D)
Cardinale Benítez: due voti. Cardinali a cui è stato assegnato un solo voto: quattro voti.

Lawrence stands and walks to the microphone, aware of the whispered conversations around him.

LAWRENCE
(Italian)
< *My brothers, in accordance with the Apostolic Constitution, we will not stop to burn the ballot papers at this point, but instead proceed immediately to the next vote...* >

LAWRENCE
Fratelli, in conformità con la Costituzione apostolica, non ci fermeremo a bruciare le schede a questo punto, ma procederemo immediatamente al successivo scrutinio...

INT. SISTINE CHAPEL - MORNING / LATER

Again...

Pencils scratch the names of cardinals on ballot papers...

Elderly cardinals labour down the aisle, ballots held aloft in shaking hands...

Ballot papers are dropped into the urn...

A needle pierces a ballot paper with scarlet thread...

Lawrence holds his pen, tip down, on his desk, waiting for the results. Cardinal Lombardi leans into the microphone.

CARDINAL LOMBARDI
(Italian)
< *The results of the third ballot are... Cardinal Adeyemi: fifty-two votes...*>

CARDINAL LOMBARDI
I risultati del terzo scrutinio sono i seguenti. Cardinale Adeyemi: cinquantadue voti...

Lawrence glances at Adeyemi. The Nigerian has his head sunk on his chest in prayer.

CARDINAL LOMBARDI (CONT'D)
< *...Cardinal Tedesco: thirty votes. Cardinal...* >

CARDINAL LOMBARDI (CONT'D)
...Cardinale Tedesco: trenta voti. Cardinale...

The pen in his hand suddenly vibrates. A faint tremor runs through the sound-proofed chamber. Lombardi, feeling it, hesitates. The rows of cardinals stir. Lombardi, puzzled, looks to Lawrence, who frowns, nods him to continue...

CARDINAL LOMBARDI (CONT'D)
(Resuming)
< Cardinal Tremblay: ten votes. Cardinal Bellini: nine votes. Cardinal Lawrence: five votes. Cardinal Benitez two votes. >

CARDINAL LOMBARDI (CONT'D)
(Resuming)
Cardinale Tremblay: dieci voti. Cardinale Bellini: nove voti. Cardinale Lawrence: cinque voti. Cardinale Benítez due voti.

INT. CASA SANTA MARTA - KITCHEN CORRIDOR - DAY

Two NUNS stand at a window, staring out at the city beyond. A sinister thread of black smoke is rising from somewhere in the east, on the Quirinal Hill. Distantly we hear the sound of sirens wailing. One of the Nuns clasps her hands and begins to pray in a low, urgent murmur. Sister Agnes appears behind them. They glance at her nervously, but from her look understand they are to continue.

INT. SALA REGIA - DAY

Lawrence walks with O'Malley. Two SECURITY MEN hurry past them.

LAWRENCE
(Quietly)
I take it something has happened?

MONSIGNOR O'MALLEY
There's been an explosion your Eminence. In the Piazza Barberini.

LAWRENCE
Dear God. A bomb?

MONSIGNOR O'MALLEY
It's unclear at this moment. There are injuries but no talk of fatalities so far.

Lawrence considers for a moment.

LAWRENCE
Say nothing to the cardinal-electors about this Ray. We are sequestered and they must be shielded from any news of the outside world in case it influences their judgement. You understand?

MONSIGNOR O'MALLEY
Of course your Eminence.

They walk on in silence.

INT. CASA SANTA MARTA - DINING ROOM - DAY

The cardinals at lunch. Some surreptitiously look to the windows, searching the skies for the dispersing veil of distant smoke.

Lawrence comes with a plate from the buffet, hesitates, then takes a seat at Bellini's table. The two men avoid each other's gaze. The other cardinals continue their stilted conversation - everyone aware that *something* has happened in the outside world.

CARDINAL VILLANUEVA
Well, it would seem that Adeyemi will be Pope before the day is out.

No-one answers for a moment.

CARDINAL VILLANUEVA (CONT'D)
I suppose the first black Pope will be a tremendous thing for the world.

CARDINAL SABBADIN
What am I supposed to tell them in Milan when they start to discover our new Pope's social views?

Lawrence is suddenly aware of a Cardinal at his shoulder. It is Guttoso.

GUTTOSO (Quietly, Italian) *< Dean, this morning's incident. Have you heard any...? >*	GUTTOSO (Quietly) *Decano, l'incidente di stamattina. Avete sentito qualcosa ...?*
LAWRENCE (Interrupting, Italian) *< Your Eminence, we are sequestered. >*	LAWRENCE (Interrupting, Italian) *Eminenza, siamo in isolamento.*
GUTTOSO *< Of course, but as a Roman myself... >*	GUTTOSO *Certo, ma essendo io stesso romano...*

LAWRENCE
(Firmly)
< I'm sorry. Paragraph four of the Apostolic Constitution is quite clear. >

LAWRENCE
(Firmly)
Mi dispiace. Il quarto paragrafo della Costituzione Apostolica è piuttosto chiaro in proposito.

Guttoso hesitates then, disgruntled, nods and walks away. Lawrence turns back to the table aware that the others have been listening. There is a beat of embarrassed silence. Then Bellini steps in, as if there had been no interruption.

BELLINI
Tell your congregation in Milan to celebrate the first African pontiff in the history of the Church.

CARDINAL SABBADIN
If Adeyemi was white we'd all be condemning him as more reactionary then Tedesco. It's only because he's...

BELLINI
(Sharp)
Enough! It's too late for this talk now.

His eyes flick to Lawrence and away again.

BELLINI (CONT'D)
All too late.

Lawrence is no longer listening. Under the chatter of the room he is puzzled to discern a raised voice. Suddenly there is a crash. He turns, in time to see a NUN hurrying back to the kitchens, followed by two more SISTERS as Adeyemi leaves his table and heads out of the room.

LAWRENCE
What happened?

Beside him, Landolfi shrugs, disinterested.

CARDINAL LANDOLFI
She dropped a bottle of wine.

No-one is paying much attention. A Nun appears with mop and bucket to clear up the mess. Lawrence looks at Adeyemi's empty chair.

INT. CASA SANTA MARTA - DINING ROOM BUFFET - DAY

Lawrence stands getting coffee. He turns and finds three of the African Cardinals behind him, their expressions mournful. And his heart sinks. For a moment he has a mad impulse to flee. But...

CARDINAL NAKITANDA
May we have a word, Dean?

LAWRENCE
Of course.

CARDINAL NAKITANDA
Our brother Joshua is troubled.

LAWRENCE
What just happened?

The cardinals exchange glances.

CARDINAL NAKITANDA
One of the nuns serving our table started talking to him. He tried to ignore her and then she dropped her tray and shouted something. He got up and left.

LAWRENCE
What did she say to him?

CARDINAL NAKITANDA
We don't know. She was speaking Yoruba.

LAWRENCE
Where is Cardinal Adeyemi now?

Nakitanda shrugs, takes his arm.

CARDINAL NAKITANDA
Clearly something is wrong, Dean, and he must tell us what. We have waited a long time for an African Pope. But he must be pure in heart and conscience. Anything less would be a disaster for us all.

INT. CASA SANTA MARTA - KITCHEN - DAY

The kitchen is full of NUNS preparing food. Lawrence crosses towards the back, looking for the missing nun. Those closest to him bow their heads as he passes.

In the back the office is empty. Lawrence returns.

LAWRENCE
(Italian)
< Could you tell me, where is the sister who just had the accident? >

LAWRENCE
Potreste dirmi dove si trova la sorella che ha fatto cadere la bottiglia prima?

NUN
(Italian)
< She is with Sister Agnes, Your Eminence. >

NUN
È con Suor Agnes, Vostra Eminenza.

LAWRENCE
< Would you be kind enough to take me to her? >

LAWRENCE
Sareste così gentile da portarmi da lei?

The Nun begins to lead him back to the dining room.

LAWRENCE (CONT'D)
< Is there a rear exit we can use? >

LAWRENCE (CONT'D)
C'è un'uscita posteriore che possiamo usare?

INT. CASA SANTA MARTA - OUTSIDE BACK OFFICE - DAY

The Nun knocks on the door of the office. There is no reply. Lawrence steps forward and knocks more loudly. After a moment, the door opens a little and SISTER AGNES peers out.

LAWRENCE
Good afternoon, Sister. I need to speak to the nun who dropped her tray just now.

SISTER AGNES
She is safe with me, Your Eminence. I am dealing with the situation.

LAWRENCE
I am sure you are Sister Agnes. But I must see her myself.

SISTER AGNES
I hardly think a dropped tray should concern the Dean of the College of Cardinals.

LAWRENCE
Even so...

He grips the door handle. Amazed, he finds that as he pushes, she resists.

SISTER AGNES
The welfare of the Sister is *my* responsibility, Dean.

An impasse as both stare at each other.

LAWRENCE
(Icy)
And this Conclave is mine.

Beat. Finally she stands aside.

INT. CASA SANTA MARTA - BACK OFFICE - DAY

The NUN - a plump middle-aged Nigerian woman - sits in a corner of the office. She stands as Lawrence enters.

LAWRENCE
Please, sit, my child. My name is Cardinal Lawrence. How are you feeling?

SISTER AGNES
She's feeling much better.

LAWRENCE
(To the Nun)
Could you tell me your name?

SISTER AGNES
Her name is Shanumi.

LAWRENCE
(To the Nun)
Please, do sit down.

SISTER AGNES
Eminence, I really do think it would be better if...

LAWRENCE
(Without looking at her)
Would you be so good as to leave us now, Sister Agnes?

She opens her mouth to protest again but Lawrence turns and stares at her with a look of such freezing authority that she finally bows her head and walks out of the room, closing the door after her. Lawrence sits, facing SISTER SHANUMI.

LAWRENCE (CONT'D)
Sister Shanumi, I want you to understand, first of all, that you are not in any sort of trouble. The fact of the matter is, I have a responsibility before God to make sure that the decisions we make here are the right ones. Now it's important that you tell me anything that is in your heart and that is troubling you in so far as it relates to Cardinal Adeyemi. Can you do that for me.

Shanumi stares at the floor, shakes her head.

LAWRENCE (CONT'D)
Even if I give you absolute assurance that it will go no further than this room?

Again, she shakes her head. Lawrence sits, at a loss. Then, inspiration strikes. He leans towards her again.

LAWRENCE (CONT'D)
Would you like me to hear your confession?

INT. CASA SANTA MARTA - CORRIDOR - DAY

TRACKING with Lawrence as he walks determinedly down the corridor.

He reaches the door of Adeyemi's room - the room next to his own and knocks. After a moment Adeyemi opens the door, drying his face.

ADEYEMI
I'll be ready in a moment, Dean.

He walks back into the room. Lawrence hesitates, then follows him...

INT. CASA SANTA MARTA - ADEYEMI'S ROOM - CONTINUOUS

Adeyemi is in the bathroom. We hear the steady stream of urination, followed by the flush. He walks out, buttoning his cassock, seems surprised to find LAWRENCE there.

ADEYEMI
Shouldn't we be leaving?

LAWRENCE
In a moment.

ADEYEMI
That sounds ominous.
(Studying himself in the mirror)
If this is about the incident downstairs, I have no desire to talk about it.

Lawrence watches in silence, waiting him out. Adeyemi turns from the mirror and walks past Lawrence into the room.

ADEYEMI (CONT'D)
I am the victim of a disgraceful plot to ruin my reputation. Someone brought that woman here and staged this melodrama. She'd never left Nigeria before and suddenly she is here in the Casa Santa Marta?

LAWRENCE
With respect, Joshua, how she came here is secondary to the issue of your relationship with her.

ADEYEMI
(turning)
I have no relationship to her! I hadn't set eyes on her for thirty years until she turned up outside my room last night!

He catches himself.

ADEYEMI (CONT'D)
It was...it was...
(Helplessly)
A *lapse*, Dean. A *lapse*! "Let God grant us a Pope who sins and asks forgiveness, and carries on." Your words!

LAWRENCE
And have you asked forgiveness?

ADEYEMI
I confessed my sin at the time! My bishop moved me to another parish and I never lapsed again! Such relationships were not uncommon in those days. You know that!

LAWRENCE
(Quietly)
And the child?

Adeyemi flinches.

ADEYEMI
The child? The child was brought up in a Christian household, and to this day he has no idea who his father is - if indeed it is me. *That* is the child.

For a moment the two men stare at each other in silence, Adeyemi's jaw jutted in defiance. Then something in him crumbles. He sits on the bed.

ADEYEMI (CONT'D)
(Beat. Broken)
We were very young.

LAWRENCE
No, Your Eminence. *She* was very young. Nineteen years old. *You* were thirty.

ADEYEMI
Thomas, *please*... Listen to me. I sensed the presence of the Holy Spirit this morning. I swear it. I am *ready* to take this burden. Does a single mistake thirty years ago disqualify me? I was a different man! I beg you, please don't use this to ruin me.

LAWRENCE
(sadly)
Joshua...the thought is not worthy of you. The woman will not speak of this to protect her son, and I am bound by the vows of the confessional.

Adeyemi looks up at him.

ADEYEMI
So... I still have hope?

Lawrence hesitates, hating this duty. He steps closer, taking Adeyemi's hands in his.

LAWRENCE
(Gently)
No, Joshua. There is no hope. After such a public scene, there will be rumours. And you know what the Curia is like. Nothing terrifies our colleagues more than the thought of yet more sexual scandals.

Adeyemi's eyes prick with tears.

LAWRENCE (CONT'D)
(Moved)
I am more sorry than I can say. You will never be Pope. You *must* begin again.

He bends closer, grips the Nigerian's hands tighter.

LAWRENCE (CONT'D)
(Fiercely)
But you are a *good* man. And you *will* find a way to atone.

A long beat. Adeyemi nods blindly, disengages his hands to wipe his eyes. He breathes deeply, gathers himself.

ADEYEMI
Will you...will you pray with me?

Beat. Lawrence holds out a hand, helps the Nigerian sink to his knees then joins him. They pray.

EXT. VATICAN GARDENS - DAY

HIGH ANGLE

...watching the tiny figure of Lawrence below us, walking through the formal geometries of the gardens. He joins Nakitanda and his two colleagues on a seat. We watch them talk for a moment. Nakitanda drops his head in dismay.

INT. SISTINE CHAPEL - DAY

The Fourth and Fifth Ballots in progress. We're watching Adeyemi walk down the aisle, his ballot held high in his hand. He passes the seats of the African Cardinals who, to a man, avert their eyes. He reaches the microphone.

ADEYEMI
(Solemnly, in Latin)
< *I call as my witness Christ the Lord, who will be my judge, that my vote is given to the one who before God I think should be elected.* >

ADEYEMI
(Solemnly)
Testor Christum Dominum, qui me iudicaturus est, me eum eligere, quem secundum Deum iudico eligi debere.

Lawrence sits, marvelling at the man's dignity in the face of his ruined life.

He turns back to his own ballot paper. A beat. Reluctantly, he writes: *Bellini.*

- Cardinals shuffle down the aisle, ballots held up in shaking hands...

- Ballots are dropped into the Urn...

- High above, the Last Judgement lies cloaked in darkness...

HARD CUT TO:

INT. SISTINE CHAPEL - DAY / LATER

Cardinal Lombardi is reading the results.

CARDINAL LOMBARDI
(Italian)
< *The results of the Fifth Ballot are... Cardinal Tremblay, forty votes.* >

CARDINAL LOMBARDI
I risultati del quinto scrutinio sono i seguenti. Cardinale Tremblay: quaranta voti.

The Canadian bows his head and places his hands together, as his colleagues twist in their seats to examine the new front-runner.

CARDINAL LOMBARDI (CONT'D)
(Italian)
< *Cardinal Tedesco, thirty-four votes. Cardinal Bellini, thirteen votes. Cardinal Lawrence, eleven votes. Cardinal Adeyemi, six votes...* >

CARDINAL LOMBARDI (CONT'D)
Cardinale Tedesco: trentaquattro voti. Cardinale Bellini: tredici voti. Cardinale Lawrence: undici voti. Cardinale Adeyemi: sei voti...

You can feel the electric tension in the room now - a staggering haemorrhage of Adeyemi's followers. In a sea of scratching pencils, the Nigerian sits staring at the wall ahead, as if oblivious.

CARDINAL LOMBARDI (CONT'D)
(Italian)
< *Cardinal Benitez, four votes.* >

CARDINAL LOMBARDI (CONT'D)
Cardinal Benítez: quattro voti.

Lawrence sits, horribly aware of being an object of curiosity for the cardinals around him, who are registering his increased share of votes. He can't stop himself looking to Bellini and finds the cardinal's cold gaze upon him.

LOMBARDI
(Italian)
< *My brothers, that concludes the fifth ballot. No candidate having achieved the necessary majority, we shall resume voting tomorrow morning.* >

LOMBARDI
Fratelli, qui si conclude il quinto scrutinio. Poiché nessun candidato ha ottenuto la maggioranza necessaria, le votazioni riprenderanno domani mattina.

INT. SISTINE CHAPEL - VESTIBULE - EVENING

The chapel has emptied. O'Malley bundles the ballots into the stove and burns them. He crosses the vestibule and turns to where Lawrence sits in the chapel, lost in thought, picks up his clipboard of notes.

LAWRENCE
(Noticing)
Yes, Ray?

MONSIGNOR O'MALLEY
The incident this morning, your Eminence. I have more information, if...?

Lawrence considers, finally shakes his head.

LAWRENCE
No, Ray. I too must be shielded from any knowledge which could act as an...*interference* in the process of this Conclave.

MONSIGNOR O'MALLEY
(Bowing)
Of course, Eminence.

LAWRENCE
Anything else?

O'Malley glances at his clipboard.

MONSIGNOR O'MALLEY
Uhh...Oh, Cardinal Benitez. His health problems? He was issued with a return ticket to Geneva, paid for from the Pope's own account. I checked the visa application. The purpose for travel was given as "medical treatment." Anyway, whatever it was, it can't have been serious. The tickets were cancelled. He never went.

Lawrence nods, barely listening.

LAWRENCE
Alright. Thank you, Ray.

O'Malley lingers. Lawrence gives him a questioning look.

MONSIGNOR O'MALLEY
(Hesitantly)
Forgive me. I know you said we should forget the matter of the withdrawn report but...I wondered in light of Cardinal Tremblay's present...position? I could see if there was anything more I could find out?

Lawrence feels a flush of anger.

LAWRENCE
I'm not a Witchfinder. It isn't my job to go hunting for secrets in my colleagues' pasts!

O'Malley nods, taken aback. Beat. Lawrence relents, touches O'Malley's wrist.

LAWRENCE (CONT'D)
I'm sorry, Ray. No more investigations. I think we've heard enough secrets.
(Standing)
Let God's Will be done.

MONSIGNOR O'MALLEY
Good night then, Your Eminence.

He watches the older man walk away.

INT. CASA SANTA MARTA - LAWRENCE'S ROOM - NIGHT

Lawrence sits on his bed, struggling to unlace his shoes. He manages to remove one and has to pause to regain his breath.

A KNOCK at the door jerks him upright and startled. He crosses to the door and opens it to reveal Bellini and Sabbadin outside.

BELLINI
Thomas.

INT. CASA SANTA MARTA - BACK STAIRS - NIGHT

Lawrence, Bellini and Sabbadin stand in a staircase.

CARDINAL SABBADIN
(Hushed)
We need to decide how we are going to proceed.

Lawrence glances around at the shadowy staircase. This feels absurd.

LAWRENCE
Is this really necessary? I feel as if I'm at some American political convention.

CARDINAL SABBADIN
(Gloomily)
Well, it isn't going to take long. Our friend here does not have sufficient support amongst our colleagues to be elected Pope.

LAWRENCE
It isn't over yet.

Bellini stirs.

BELLINI
(Heavily)
I'm afraid, as far as I'm concerned, it is. The question arises, if I can't win, whom should I advise my supporters to vote for?

He clears his throat. An awkward beat.

BELLINI (CONT'D)
Obviously there is you. But...

CARDINAL SABBADIN
(Bluntly)
But you can't win either. Even if we delivered you all of Aldo's fifteen votes - which I don't believe we could - you'd still be in third place, behind Tremblay and Tedesco. No-one has enough traction to catch either of the front-runners. So, since we all agree that Tedesco would be a disaster...

He spreads his hands. The three stand in silence for a moment.

BELLINI
I'm no more of an enthusiast for Tremblay than you are, Thomas. But we have to face the fact that--

A few stories below a door creaks, footsteps on marble echo throughout the staircase. Bellini peers over the banister at a cardinal in conversation below. He continues, lowering his voice.

BELLINI (CONT'D)
He has demonstrated a broad appeal.
(Without much conviction)
Perhaps he will be a unifying force?

Lawrence shakes his head.

BELLINI (CONT'D)
What?

LAWRENCE
Is this what we are reduced to? Considering the "least-worst" option?

BELLINI
(Irritated)
The field has narrowed. If we don't change our votes, we'll be here for weeks. Which is what Tedesco wants.

LAWRENCE
(Beat)
I have been informed that, shortly before his death, the Holy Father had fallen out with Tremblay. In fact, that he intended to dismiss him from all offices in the Church.

The two stare at him, stunned.

LAWRENCE (CONT'D)
There is a rumour of a report of some kind, a report that was possibly withdrawn...

Sabbadin glances nervously at Bellini, who frowns.

BELLINI
A rumour?
(Beat)
Thomas, in the last weeks of his life it is possible that the Holy Father was not entirely *himself.* He had become increasingly secretive and paranoid...

CARDINAL SABBADIN
(Joining in)
Even if there *was* a report...

They turn to look at him.

CARDINAL SABBADIN (CONT'D)
What I mean is...We've had a Pope who was in the Hitler Youth and fought for the Nazis. We've had Popes accused of colluding with communists and fascists. We've had Popes who have ignored reports of the most appalling sexual abuse of children...

BELLINI
(Impatient)
We take the point...

CARDINAL SABBADIN
The point is - we will *never* find a candidate who doesn't have some kind of black mark against them! We are mortal men! We serve an ideal - we cannot always *be* ideal.

Beat. Lawrence looks at his friend, but Bellini avoids his gaze.

BELLINI
(Flat)
So we're agreed. We urge all our supporters to back Tremblay.

The three stand in silence - the gloom of *realpolitik* descending upon them.

INT. CASA SANTA MARTA - LIFT - NIGHT

Lawrence stands lost in thought as the elevator rises. It stops at a floor and the doors slide open.

The ancient Cardinal LOWENSTEIN, grey-faced with fatigue, leaning on his walking stick, creeps slowly into the lift. Lawrence bites down on his impatience, flashes a smile, holding the door for his elderly colleague.

On the landing beyond a door opens <u>and Tedesco and Adeyemi emerge from a room.</u>

Adeyemi and Lawrence lock gazes. The Nigerian's former sorrow and remorse seems to have passed, to be replaced by a look of defiance, almost hostility. Then he turns away, following the Patriarch of Venice.

OMITTED

INT. CASA SANTA MARTA - LIFT - NIGHT

The doors slide closed again and the elevator continues its ascent. For a moment the only sound is Lowenstein's laboured breathing. Then...

CARDINAL LOWENSTEIN
If this drags on much longer I might die before we find a new Pope.

Lawrence is still thinking about what he's just seen - the formation of a new right-wing voting block?

LAWRENCE
(Grimly)
Then let's try to finish it.

INT. CASA SANTA MARTA - UPPER CORRIDOR - NIGHT

A door opens a little and Benitez peers cautiously out at us, his open cassock clutched together at his throat.

BENITEZ
Your Eminence?

Lawrence is a little taken aback by Benitez' wariness.

LAWRENCE
I'm sorry to disturb you. May I have a word?

BENITEZ
Of course. One moment.

To Thomas' surprise, Benitez disappears back into the room, leaving him standing in the corridor. After a moment he reappears, clothed now.

BENITEZ (CONT'D)
(Ushering him in)
Excuse me, at this time of day I always try to meditate for an hour...

INT. CASA SANTA MARTA - BENITEZ ROOM - CONTINUOUS

Lawrence takes in the room - identical to his own, except for a few lit candles here and the bathroom beyond.

BENITEZ
(Apologetically)
In my travels I became used to not always having electricity. Now I find it helpful when I pray alone.

LAWRENCE
(Politely)
I must see if it helps me.

BENITEZ
Yes. Your difficulty with prayer.

He watches Lawrence, the same keen gaze. Lawrence nods.

BENITEZ (CONT'D)
(Gently)
If I may say... sometimes I find, instead of speaking, I have to become silent. And in the silence wait for God to be heard.

For a moment Lawrence feels affronted - is he, the Dean, to be given lessons in prayer now? But he fights it down.

LAWRENCE
Yes. I'm sure you're right.

BENITEZ
Excuse me...

He sits and starts to tie his shoes.

LAWRENCE
The other night you were kind enough to say you had voted for me. I don't know if you've continued to do so, but if you have I would like to repeat my plea to you to stop.

BENITEZ
Why?

LAWRENCE
First, because I lack the spiritual depth to be Pope. And secondly I can't possibly win. A long drawn out Conclave would be seen by the media as proof that the Church is in crisis.

BENITEZ
You have come to ask me to vote for Cardinal Tremblay?

LAWRENCE
Yes. And to urge your supporters to do the same.

BENITEZ
Cardinal Tremblay has already spoken to me about this.

LAWRENCE
(Bitterly)
I'm sure he has.

He regrets his tone instantly. Benitez studies him solemnly.

BENITEZ
You want me to vote for a man you see as ambitious?

LAWRENCE
I do not want to see Tedesco as Pope. He would take the Church back to an earlier era.

BENITEZ
I'm sorry. I cannot vote for a man unless he is the one I deem most worthy to be Pope. And for me, that is not Cardinal Tremblay. It is you.

Lawrence strikes the side of his seat in frustration.

LAWRENCE
I don't *want* your vote!

Benitez stares back at him calmly, and once more Lawrence senses a surprising strength of character in this frail man.

BENITEZ
(Calmly)
Never the less, you have it.

He walks towards the bathroom, blowing out a few candles.

Lawrence watches for a moment and then sighs. He wets thumb and forefinger and snuffs out the candle beside the bed. As he does he stares, distracted, at the little razor, out of place in the bedroom, still in its cellophane wrapper. And wonders why he has noted this.

OMITTED

INT. CASA SANTA MARTA - DINING ROOM - NIGHT

Tedesco sits, holding court with his supporters. Adeyemi and the African cardinals sit with him now.

On the other side of the room, Tremblay circulates amongst his supporters, shaking hands, exchanging a few remarks, every inch the political campaigner.

Lawrence sits watching the two factions, sick at heart. His gaze drifts to the blue-habited nuns moving between the tables with trays and wine, eyes downcast.

On a sudden impulse, he stands.

INT. CASA SANTA MARTA - BACK OFFICE - NIGHT

Lawrence sits with Sister Agnes, her eyes darting to the cage with the canary.

SISTER AGNES
Sister Shanumi is on her way home to Nigeria.
(Off Thomas' look)
There was a flight to Lagos this evening. I thought it was best for everyone if she was on it.

LAWRENCE
(Beat. Quietly)
How did Sister Shanumi come to be in Rome?

SISTER AGNES
I received notification from the office of the Superioress General that she would be joining us. The arrangements were made in Paris. You should ask the Rue de Bac, Your Eminence.

LAWRENCE
I would, except that, as you know, I am sequestered for the duration of the Conclave.

SISTER AGNES
Then you can ask them afterwards.

LAWRENCE
The information is of value to me now.

Sister Agnes stares at him, her indomitable gaze. She gets up and checks on the bird which has been oddly silent.

LAWRENCE (CONT'D)
I know you were close to the late Pope. When I tried to resign as dean, the Holy Father wouldn't let me. I didn't understand why at the time. But now I think I understand. I think he knew he was dying and for some reason he wanted me to run this Conclave. And that is what I'm trying to do. For *him.*

Sister Agnes turns and stares at him in silence for a moment. Then she puts her glasses on and turns to the computer on the desk. She types rapidly, then stands and walks away, leaving Lawrence to view the e-mail she has opened up. It is marked *October 3rd, Confidential*. Lawrence's gaze is drawn to the last paragraph...

"...I would be grateful if you could take particular care of our sister, as her presence has been requested by the Prefect of the Congregation for the Evangelisation of Peoples, His Eminence, Cardinal Joseph Tremblay."

Lawrence stares at the name.

INT. CASA SANTA MARTA - STAIRCASE - NIGHT

After dinner Cardinals are heading for the stairs and elevator. Tremblay amongst a group of acolytes.

LAWRENCE (O.S.)
Your Eminence, a word if I may?

Tremblay turns -- Lawrence stands on the staircase above him, waiting.

TREMBLAY
(Smiling)
I was just on my way to bed.

LAWRENCE
It won't take a moment. Come.

Tremblay's smile is suddenly wary as Lawrence leads him to...

EXT. CASA SANTA MARTA - COURTYARD CORRIDOR - NIGHT

The corridor is empty and in semi-darkness. Tremblay and Lawrence stand in the light of the fluorescents, their breath pluming in the air.

TREMBLAY
(still smiling)
I know you enjoy mystery novels
Thomas but this is...

LAWRENCE
I want you to withdraw your name
from the next ballot.

Tremblay sighs, shakes his head with a sorrowful smile.

LAWRENCE (CONT'D)
You are not the right man to be Pope.

TREMBLAY
Well, forty of our colleagues would disagree with you, so...

LAWRENCE
Only because they don't know you as I do.

Tremblay looks genuinely shocked at the remark.

TREMBLAY
This is sad, Thomas. I shall pray for you and...

LAWRENCE
(Over)
I know there was some kind of report into your activities. I know the Holy Father raised the matter with you hours before he died and that he dismissed you from all your posts. And I know that, somehow, you discovered Adeyemi's surrender to temptation thirty years ago and arranged for the woman involved to be brought to Rome, with the express intention of destroying Adeyemi's chance of becoming Pope.

TREMBLAY
I deny that accusation.

LAWRENCE
You deny asking our Superioress to transfer one of her sisters to Rome?

TREMBLAY
No. I asked her - but not on my own behalf.

LAWRENCE
On whose behalf, then?

TREMBLAY
The Holy Father's.

Lawrence stares at him, staggered.

LAWRENCE
You would *libel* the Holy Father in his own home?

TREMBLAY
It isn't libel, it's the truth! The Holy Father gave me the name of a sister and asked me to make a private request to bring her to Rome. I had no idea why. And you...
(Stepping closer)
You should be careful Thomas. Your own ambition has not gone unnoticed. This might be seen as a tactic to blacken the name of a rival.

LAWRENCE
That is a despicable accusation.

TREMBLAY
Is it? I wonder if you really *are* so very reluctant to have the chalice passed to you!

He makes a visible effort to catch his anger.

TREMBLAY (CONT'D)
I shall pretend this conversation never took place.

He walks away.

LAWRENCE
(After him, impotent anger)
But it *has* taken place!

Across the courtyard a security guard smokes a cigarette. Alone in the dark, Lawrence feels his uncomfortable gaze upon him.

INT. CASA SANTA MARTA - LAWRENCE'S ROOM - NIGHT

The only source of light shining from the bathroom Lawrence lies on his bed, praying. After a moment his eyes open and he stares blindly ahead, hoping for some sign, some guidance... The sound of Adeyemi's snoring coming from next door.

Suddenly Lawrence sits up in bed, a decision forming in his mind. He opens the drawer to his nightstand... taking the pass key Sister Agnes had lent him.

OMITTED

INT. CASA SANTA MARTA - PAPAL CORRIDOR - NIGHT

At the end of the corridor the lift doors open, a silhouette appearing in the hall. Lawrence silently walks down the empty corridor.

In front of the papal suite the votive candles flicker in their red glasses. The locked door is still criss-crossed with red ribbons.

Lawrence stares at the door, building his courage. Then he takes Sister Agnes' pass key and unlocks the door. He hesitates then pushes the door open, the wax seals cracking free and the ribbons fluttering down...

Lawrence crosses himself and then steps into...

INT. PAPAL SUITE - NIGHT

Lawrence fumbles on the light and stares around the familiar, plain room, the few simple items of furniture: the blue scalloped sofa and matching armchairs, the coffee table, the prie-dieu.

INT. PAPAL OFFICE - NIGHT

Lawrence sits at the desk, takes the briefcase on his knee and opens it. Inside is an electric razor, a tin of peppermints and a battered copy of The Imitation of Christ by Thomas à Kempis. An ancient bus-ticket acts as a book-mark. Lawrence opens the book and finds a passage underlined:

"At the Day of Judgement we shall not be asked what we have read but what we have done."

Lawrence stares at the words. They feel like encouragement, a command almost, from the late Holy father.

Lawrence searches through the Pope's desk, rooting through the drawers... An empty spectacles case, a plastic bottle of lens cleaner, a box of aspirin, a calculator, rubber bands...

He freezes, hearing FOOTSTEPS approach.

INT. PAPAL CORRIDOR - CONTINUOUS

SISTER AGNES is walking down the corridor. She slows, seeing the broken seals of the papal suite and the light showing beneath the door. She stops at the door, listening.

Then the LIGHT below the Papal Suite door switches off.

INT. PAPAL SUITE - CONTINUOUS

Lawrence stands by the light switch in the darkness, practically holding his breath - aware that someone is just on the other side of the door.

INT. OUTSIDE THE PAPAL SUITE - CONTINUOUS

SISTER AGNES hesitates, her hand on the door handle, considering who the intruder could be.

<u>And suddenly she is certain that it is Lawrence on the other side of the door.</u>

<u>A strange moment of connection.</u>

Then TWO NUNS cross the corridor behind her, deep in conversation in Italian, breaking the silence.

Agnes straightens up again and walks on down the corridor.

INT. PAPAL SUITE - CONTINUOUS

Lawrence waits in the dark, listening to her footsteps recede. Then he switches the light back on.

INT. PAPAL BEDROOM - MOMENTS LATER

Lawrence enters, silhouetted in the door frame. The bed has been stripped.

He opens the wardrobe - a simple closet that has been emptied of everything except two ghost-like cassocks that hang from the rail. The sight of them makes his heart ache.

He turns to the bedside cabinet, kneels carefully and checks the small drawer, but it's empty.

On top of the cabinet lie the late Pope's spectacles and alarm clock, just as they were on the night the pope died.

The sight of them finally undoes Lawrence and leans his elbows on the bed, his face in his hands, and is wracked by a fit of dry sobbing.

Finally, he opens his eyes again, bleakly accepting that he has given in to a fit of paranoid madness. He is about to stand again when he finds himself staring at the headboard with it's pitifully frayed edge, the crack in the wood, as if some implement had been forced into the join...

He reaches out a hand and pulls at the bottom corner of the padded head-piece. It resists. With both hands now he pulls harder, grunting with the effort...

The headboard inches out from its frame. The material on the inside edge, normally hidden, has a frayed six inch slit down it.

Tentatively Lawrence slips his fingers into the padded interior.

When he withdraws them he his holding several FOLDED SHEETS OF PAPER.

INT. CASA SANTA MARTA - UPPER CORRIDOR - NIGHT

Bellini opens his door and blinks at Lawrence.

INT. CASA SANTA MARTA - BELLINI'S ROOM - NIGHT

Lawrence stands sipping a glass of water. Bellini sits on the bed, reading the sheets of paper.

LAWRENCE
It's the report on the activities of Tremblay. It's an overwhelming prima facie case that he is guilty of simony - an offence that is stipulated in the Holy Scripture as...

BELLINI
(Reading)
I am aware of what simony is, thank you.

LAWRENCE
He only obtained all those votes on the first ballot because he bought them. Cardenas, Diene, Figarella, Baptiste...
(MORE)

LAWRENCE (CONT'D)
And all of this done in the last twelve months when he must have guessed the Holy Father's pontificate was coming to an end!

BELLINI
(Of the papers)
How do you know they didn't use this money for completely legitimate purposes?

LAWRENCE
Because I've seen their bank statements.

BELLINI
Dear God.

Lawrence finds himself staring down at the small plastic CHESS SET which Bellini had taken from the Pope's apartment; the pieces still grouped in the unfinished final game.

LAWRENCE
Ours too. It would seem the Holy Father was spying on all of us. I don't think he trusted anyone.

Bellini looks up from the sheets.

BELLINI
Where did you find these?

Lawrence is silent.

BELLINI (CONT'D)
(Appalled)
You broke the seals?

LAWRENCE
What choice did I have? I suspected Tremblay of bringing that poor woman from Africa to embarrass Adeyem i.

BELLINI
And did he?

LAWRENCE
He asked for the transfer. He claims he did it at the request of the Holy Father but... You must continue with your candidacy, Aldo.

Bellini stares at the papers in his hand. He holds them out to Lawrence.

BELLINI
Put them back. Put them back or burn them or... put them back.
(Off Thomas' stare)
I couldn't possibly become Pope in such circumstances, a dirty trick, a stolen document, the smearing of a brother cardinal... I'd be the Richard Nixon of Popes!

LAWRENCE
Then keep clear of this. Leave it to me. I'm willing to take the consequences and...

BELLINI
(Over)
You know who will gain most from this? Tedesco! The whole basis of his candidacy is that the Holy Father led the Church to disaster by his attempts at reform. If you reveal this report it isn't Tremblay's reputation which will suffer - it's the Church's. Accusing the Curia of institutional corruption...

LAWRENCE
I thought we were here to serve God, not the Curia...

BELLINI
Oh, don't be naive!

They stare at each other in shocked silence. Then...

BELLINI (CONT'D)
(Quietly)
Put them back.

LAWRENCE
(Beat)
And have Tremblay as Pope?

BELLINI
We've had worse.

LAWRENCE
(Beat)
What has he offered you? Secretary of State?

Beat. Bellini looks away. Lawrence studies his friend for a moment.

LAWRENCE (CONT'D)
Five times I cast my ballot for you, Aldo. But I was wrong. You lack the courage required to be Pope.

He gets up and walks out.

TITLE CARD: THIRD DAY OF CONCLAVE.

INT. CASA SANTA MARTA - SECURITY GATE - EARLY MORNING

Dawn. Security check the line of NUNS arriving to prepare breakfast. They bow their heads to a Cardinal as he passes.

INT. CASA SANTA MARTA - STORAGE ROOM - EARLY MORNING

A sheet from the REPORT is placed on the photocopier plate. The heading reads Strictly Confidential. The names of some cardinals have been obliterated with pen.

Lawrence, bleary from a sleepless night, stands staring at the array of settings. He presses a button. *"Error"* flashes on the screen. Lawrence stares at the message, wondering if it's an obscure judgement...

SISTER AGNES (O.S.)
I'll do that for you, Your Eminence.

Started, Lawrence finds Sister Agnes behind him, watching him with her unwavering gaze. She glances at the sheet, taking in that heading. Lawrence waits, frozen.

SISTER AGNES (CONT'D)
How many copies do you require?

LAWRENCE
One hundred and eight.

A fractional hesitation. Then Sister Agnes nods and moves to the copier...

INT. CASA SANTA MARTA - DINING ROOM - MORNING

Sister Agnes walks from plate to plate, distributing large brown envelopes. Cardinal Lawrence helps here the first CARDINALS arrive and take their seats at the dining tables.

INT. CASA SANTA MARTA - DINING ROOM - MORNING / LATER

The dining room is now full, the buzz of excited conversation. Cardinals turn in their seats to stare at Lawrence who sits, impassive, feeling strangely calm. Sabbadin appears in front of him, tosses the report on the table before him.

CARDINAL SABBADIN
(Hissing)
You have wasted this report! We could have used it to control Tremblay after he was elected Pope. All you have done is strengthen Tedesco.

He walks away before Lawrence can reply. Benitez sits at the table beside him with bread and fruit.

BENITEZ
You should eat Dean.

Lawrence stares blindly at the food.

LAWRENCE
Did I do the right thing, Vincent?

BENITEZ
No one who follows their conscience ever does wrong, Your Eminence.

The room falls suddenly silent as Tremblay appears, hair immaculate, chin jutted. He strides towards Lawrence.

TREMBLAY
(Loudly)
You are responsible for this I believe?

LAWRENCE
No, Your Eminence. You are.

TREMBLAY
(For the room)
This report is entirely mendacious! It would never have seen the light of day if you had not broken into the Holy Father's apartment to remove it!

LAWRENCE
(Calmly)
If the report is mendacious then why did the Holy Father, in his last official act as Pope, ask you to resign?

A stir of amazement from the listening CARDINALS.

TREMBLAY
He did no such thing! As Monsignor Morales, who was at the meeting will confirm.

LAWRENCE
And yet Archbishop Wozniak insists that the Holy Father told him personally of the conversation...

TREMBLAY
(Over)
The Holy Father - may his name be numbered among the high priests - was a sick man towards the end of his life as those of us who saw him regularly will confirm!

TEDESCO
(Standing, Italian)
< If someone else may be allowed to join this dialogue - the names of eight cardinals have been blacked out. I assume the dean can tell us who they are? Let them confirm, here and now, whether Cardinal Tremblay requested their votes in return for the payment. >

TEDESCO
(Standing)
Se è possibile aggiungere qualcun altro a questa conversazione... i nomi di otto cardinali sono stati oscurati. Immagino che il Decano possa dirci chi sono? Lasciamo che siano loro a confermare, qui ed ora, se il Cardinal Tremblay ha richiesto i loro voti in cambio di soldi.

LAWRENCE
(Beat)
No. I won't do that.

Uproar.

LAWRENCE (CONT'D)
(Almost drowned by the commotion)
Let each man examine his conscience, as I have.
(MORE)

LAWRENCE (CONT'D)
I have no desire to create bitterness in this Conclave and will be happy to stand down as dean...

More uproar. At his table, Bellini watches his old friend standing alone in the storm of voices, conflicted whether he should come to his aid, when...

SISTER AGNES (O.S.)
Your Eminences... Your Eminences...

Gradually the words cut through and the cardinals turn to stare at the small, resolute figure of Sister Agnes standing in their midst. A silence falls, perhaps out of shock at her presumption.

SISTER AGNES (CONT'D)
Eminences, although we Sisters are supposed to be invisible, God has nevertheless given us eyes and ears. I know what prompted the Dean of the College to enter the Holy Father's rooms. He was concerned that the sister from my order who made that regrettable scene might have been brought to Rome with the deliberate intention of embarrassing a member of this Conclave. His suspicions were correct. She was indeed here at the specific request of Cardinal Tremblay.

She genuflects and then walks out, head held very erect. Tremblay gapes after her in horror.

TREMBLAY
My brothers, it's true the Holy Father asked me to. I had no knowledge of who she was - I swear to you!

For a moment no-one speaks. Then Adeyemi stands and points a finger at him.

ADEYEMI
Judas.

He turns and walks out and Tremblay finds the cardinals staring at him, stony-faced.

INT. CASA SANTA MARTA - PRAYER ROOM - MORNING

Lawrence kneels in prayer. He looks up as Bellini kneels beside him. A beat.

BELLINI
(Wryly)
We seem to be running out of favourites.

LAWRENCE
You should take over the supervision of this election, Aldo.

BELLINI
Ha! No, thank you. You are steering this Conclave. Exactly *where* I do not know, but you are certainly steering it. And that firm hand of yours has its admirers. (Beat) I've come to ask your forgiveness.

Surprised, Lawrence looks at him.

BELLINI (CONT'D)
I had the temerity to tell you to examine your heart, when all the time my own was...

He shakes his head.

BELLINI (CONT'D)
Shameful to be this age and still not know yourself.
(A rueful smile)
Ambition, "the moth of holiness."
(Beat)
Perhaps it's time you decided upon a name?

Lawrence stares at him.

BELLINI (CONT'D)
As the next most senior member of the Conclave, it will fall to me to ask you how you wish to be known as Pope. Rightly or wrongly, it would seem Tremblay is finished. This will be a contest between Tedesco and you. You're the only one who can stop him now.

The two old friends stare at each other. Then, as if admitting to himself for the first time that the thought, the *ambition*, was always there...

LAWRENCE
John. I would choose John.

Beat. Then Bellini nods.

BELLINI
It has a weight to it.

OMITTED

INT. SISTINE CHAPEL - DAY

A BLANK BALLOT.

Lawrence stares at his own sheet, for the first time at a loss as to which name to write. He closes his eyes, hoping for inspiration, some sign. Nothing comes. He opens his eyes, looks up...

And finds Tedesco watching him. The Patriarch raises his eyebrows in amused complicity: *Just you and me.*

Lawrence picks up his pen, feeling he no longer has a choice. Slowly he writes a name on the ballot. “Lawrence.”

He stands and holding the ballot above his head, walks down the aisle to the waiting chalice, knowing he is about to sin.

LAWRENCE
(in Latin)
< I call as my witness Christ the Lord, who will be my judge, that my vote is given before God to the one who I think should be elected. >

LAWRENCE
Testor Christum Dominum, qui me iudicaturus est, me eum eligere, quem secundum Deum iudico eligi debere.

He holds the ballot over the chalice. Hesitates.

Then he drops the ballot into the chalice.

The explosion is felt first as a ripple in the floor, a bass vibration throughout his body. Then the boarded windows are blasted in, raining glass down onto the chapel.

For a moment Lawrence stands, stunned, wondering, almost hoping, that he is dead. Time slows.

For the first time bright morning light floods the former gloom of the chapel and Lawrence finds himself dwarfed and pitiful before Michelangelo's vast fresco The Last Judgement. The work burns brilliantly before him, Christ dividing the Damned from the Saved...

He turns again and finds the doors at the end of the vestibule beginning to open, screeching across the glass-strewn floor.

INT. SISTINE CHAPEL - VESTIBULE - DAY

Two SECURITY GUARDS, guns drawn, begin to push their way in. Frightened faces peer from behind them.

INT. PAULINE CHAPEL - DAY

CLOSE ON A FRESCO - Michelangelo's *Crucifixion of St Peter*.

Lawrence stands, staring at the huge fresco. St Peter, about to be crucified upside down, cranes his neck upward, eyes us reproachfully.

O'Malley pads down the chapel and joins him.

MONSIGNOR O'MALLEY
Everyone has been taken to the Casa Santa Marta, Your Eminence. No one was seriously hurt. Some cuts, that's all.

Lawrence stares at the fresco for a moment.

LAWRENCE
(Without looking at him)
And outside? In the city? How bad is it?

O'Malley passes him a s heet of paper. Lawrence reads it.

LAWRENCE (CONT'D)
(Softly)
Dear God.

O'Malley examines his exhausted face.

MONSIGNOR O'MALLEY
How are you feeling?

LAWRENCE
(Beat)
I was looking at the darkness at the top of the painting.

LAWRENCE (CONT'D)
I used to think they were clouds. But I think it's smoke. There's a fire somewhere. Some violence. And St Peter, straining to keep his head upright.

O'Malley hesitates, wondering if Lawrence is in shock.

MONSIGNOR O'MALLEY
Your Eminence? The Conclave? Do we continue?

Lawrence doesn't know what to say.

I/E. POLICE CAR - DAY

Lawrence stares out from the back of the car as it speeds through the courtyards of the Vatican, siren blaring, the startled faces of the Swiss Guards they pass, bathed in pulsing blue light.

He glances up at the sky, watching the helicopter that buzzes angrily overhead, missiles protruding from its belly.

EXT. CASA SANTA MARTA - LOBBY - DAY

PUSHING LAWRENCE as he strides into the Casa, sweeps through the courtyard, past frightened groups of NUNS and CURIA. Mandorff waits for him.

LAWRENCE
(As he passes him)
Complete privacy, Willi.

Mandorff nods grimly and follows him towards the Casa...

INT. CASA SANTA MARTA - AULA - DAY

The assembled cardinals look up anxiously from their seats.

LAWRENCE
My brothers, I would like to have the authority of the Conclave to discuss what has happened.

Archbishop Krasinski, a Tedesco supporter, stands.

KRASINSKI
Paragraph four of the constitution states that nothing can be done in the College of Cardinals that "in any way affects the procedures governing the election of the Supreme Pontiff." The very fact that you are holding this meeting outside the Sistine Chapel *is* an interference!

Beside Lawrence, Bellini is already on his feet.

BELLINI
It's quite clear that something serious *has* occurred and I for one would like to know what it is.

TEDESCO
(Italian)
You *are* merely *looking* for an excuse to delay the decision!
(English)
We are here to listen to God, not news bulletins.

BELLINI
No doubt you think we shouldn't listen to explosions either, but we all heard one!

There is a murmur of approval and Tedesco colours. Lawrence seizes the moment.

LAWRENCE
Will all those who wish the Conclave to receive this information, please raise their hands?

Scores of hands are raised - a clear majority.

LAWRENCE (CONT'D)
Very well.

LAWRENCE (CONT'D)
(Reading from the sheet of paper)
At eleven twenty this morning, a car bomb exploded in the Piazza del Risorgimento.
(MORE)

LAWRENCE (CONT'D)
Shortly afterwards, as people were fleeing the scene, an individual with explosives strapped to his body detonated himself. There are reports of further attacks in Louvain and Munich...

A ripple of dismay is spreading throughout the room.

LAWRENCE (CONT'D)
The current death toll stands at fifty two. Hundreds have been injured.

The expressions of horror grow in volume. Tedesco lumbers to his feet again hand raised like an Old Testament prophet, something horribly triumphant in his manner.

TEDESCO
(Italian)
< *Here! Here we see the result of the doctrine of relativism so beloved of our liberal brothers! A relativism that sees all faiths and passing fancies accorded equal weight, so that now, when we look around us, we see the homeland of the Holy Roman Catholic Church dotted with the mosques and minarets of Muhammad! Sembra che non ci sia più la vera Fede.* *

TEDESCO
Qui. Qui vediamo il risultato della dottrina del relativismo tanto amata dai nostri fratelli liberali! Un relativismo che vede tutte le fedi e le fantasie passeggere avere lo stesso peso, tanto che ora, quando ci guardiamo intorno, vediamo la patria della Santa Chiesa Cattolica romana punteggiata dalle moschee e dai minareti di Maometto! Sembra che non ci sia più la vera Fede.

TEDESCO (CONT'D)
(switching to English)
Perhaps there is to be no Truth at all! >

BELLINI
(English))
You should be ashamed, Tedesco!

Tedesco wheels on him, scarlet with anger - a rare moment of loss of control.

TEDESCO
(English)
Ashamed? Yes! We should ALL be ashamed!

TEDESCO (CONT'D)
(Italian)
< We tolerate Islam in our land, but they revile us in theirs! We nourish them in our homelands, but they exterminate us in theirs! And now they are literally at our walls and we do nothing! How long will we persist in this weakness...? What we need now is a leader who will accept that we are once more facing a religious war! >

TEDESCO (CONT'D)
Noi tolleriamo l'Islam nella nostra terra, ma loro ci ripudiano nella loro! Li nutriamo nella nostra patria, ma ci sterminano nella loro! E ora sono letteralmente alle nostre porte e noi non facciamo nulla! Fino a quando persisteremo in questa debolezza? Quello di cui abbiamo bisogno è di una guida che accetti che ci troviamo di nuovo di fronte a una guerra di religione!

Krasinski, sensing he is going too far, reaches up a restraining hand but Tedesco brushes him angrily aside.

TEDESCO (CONT'D)
(Italian)
< A leader who will hold fast to our traditions! A leader who will put a stop to the drift that has gone on almost ceaselessly for the past fifty years and that has rendered us so weak in the face of this evil! We need a leader who will find the strength to fight these *
animals! > *

TEDESCO (CONT'D)
Una guida che sia saldamente legata alle nostre tradizioni! Una guida che ponga fine alla deriva che continua quasi incessantemente da cinquant'anni e che ci ha reso così deboli di fronte a questo male! Abbiamo bisogno di un capo --
(in English)
-- di un leader who will find the strength to fight these animals!

BENITEZ
(to Tedesco, over the uproar)
My brother Cardinal...

The cardinals fall silent.

BENITEZ (CONT'D)
With respect... what do you know about war?

Tedesco turns to look at him in surprise.

BENITEZ (CONT'D)

I carried out my ministry in the Congo, in Baghdad and Kabul. I have seen the lines of the dead and wounded, Christian AND Muslim. When you say "we have to fight" - what is it you think we're fighting? You think it's those deluded men who have carried out these terrible acts today.
No my brother.

(continues in Spanish)

BENITEZ (CONT'D)

La lucha está aquí... aquí dentro de cada uno de nosotros si cedemos al odio y al temor, si hablamos de "bandos" en vez de hablar por cada hombre y cada mujer.

Esta es mi primera vez entre ustedes y probablemente sea mi última. Y perdónenme, pero en estos días solo hemos demostrado ser un grupo de hombres pequeños y mezquinos Interesados solamente en nosotros mismos, en Roma, en la elección y el poder.

Pero estas cosas no son la iglesia. La iglesia no es la tradición. La iglesia no es el pasado. La iglesia es lo que hagamos en adelante.

BENITEZ (CONT'D)

(in Spanish)

< The thing you're fighting is here... inside each and every one of us, if you give into hate now, if we speak of "sides" instead of speaking for every man and woman.

This is my first time amongst you and I suppose it will be my last. Forgive me, but these last few days we have shown ourselves to be small and petty men. We have seemed concerned only with ourselves, with Rome, with these elections, with power.

But these things are not the Church. The Church is not a tradition. The Church is not the past. The Church is what we do next. >

EXT. CASA SANTA MARTA - SECOND FLOOR - DAY

A nun walks quickly away from camera

INT. CASA SANTA MARTA/ EXT AULA - DAY

Cardinals exit down the steps.

INT. CASA SANTA MARTA/ EXT AULA - DAY

A group of Nuns walk quickly down a stairway.

EXT. CASA SANTA MARTA COURTYARD - DAY

Nun's walk hurriedly past Cardinals standing in small groups having animated conversations

EXT CASA SANTA MARTA COURTYARD - DAY

Many Cardinals stand in small groups having animated conversations

EXT CASA SANTA MARTA COURTYARD - DAY

Three Cardinals have a hushed conversation. Dozens of other cardinals in the background do the same.

EXT CASA SANTA MARTA COURTYARD - SECOND FLOOR - DAY

Two Nun's look at someone below. Small groups of Cardinals continue their discussions.

EXT CASA SANTA MARTA COURTYARD - SECOND FLOOR - DAY

POV of Nuns looking at scores of Cardinals gathered below talking. Cardinal Benetiz sits alone on a bench with a sandwich as other Cardinals glance at him.

EXT. CASA SANTA MARTA - PARKING - DAY

Lawrence sits alone, digesting the contentious gathering, as a light drizzle of rain hits the pavement. Archbishop Mandorff quietly approaches.

ARCHBISHOP MANDORFF
The drivers aren't ready, Your Eminence.

Lawrence tears himself away from his thoughts.

LAWRENCE
Then we shall walk, Willi.

EXT. VATICAN GARDENS - DAY

Lawrence leads the cardinals from the hostel. Overhead helicopters drone. Lawrence ignores them and opens up his umbrella. It has begun to rain.

The mass of cardinals follow, walking in silence, a sea of white umbrellas crossing the gardens.

A sense of silent solidarity. Bellini arrives beside Lawrence. He takes his arm in his. The two friends look at each other, united again. They walk on.

INT. SISTINE CHAPEL - DAY

The broken glass has been swept away. A faint breeze blows through the space where the windows were.

Lawrence stands at the microphone. The beginning of what he senses will be the final ballot of the Conclave.

LAWRENCE
(Latin)
< O Father, so that we may guide and watch over Your Church, give to us, Your servants, the blessings of intelligence, truth and peace, so that we may strive to know Your will, and serve You with total dedication. For Christ our Lord... >

LAWRENCE
Ecclesiae tuae, Domine, rector et custos, infunde, quaesumus, famulis tuis spiritum intelligentiae, veritatis et pacis, ut, quae tibi placita sunt, toto corde cognoscant et agnita tota virtute sectentur. Per Christum Dominum nostrum.

From the assembled Conclave comes the low rumble of "Amen."

ON LAWRENCE...

...sitting staring up at the painted ceiling high above. His gaze slips to the rows of cardinals, lingers a moment on Tedesco, Tremblay, Adeyemi, Benitez, Bellini... He feels a sudden wave of love for them all, in all their imperfection: *the crooked timber of humanity...*

From outside comes a strange, soft sound - the rise and fall of an immense wave. The cardinals raise their heads, listening, puzzled, until they realise: it is the sound of tens of thousands gathering in St Peter's Square.

Droplets of water are trickling through the shattered windows, and down the stone walls.

Lawrence watches the raindrops for a moment. Then he picks up his pen. His mind feels suddenly calm, clear. A moment of grace.

He begins to write.

INT. SISTINE CHAPEL - MONTAGE - DAY

...ballots fall into the waiting urn....

...the ballots are pierced by the needle, threaded on the scarlet strand.

...the hands of the Scrutineers take ballots from the urn and pass it along...

...the white cloth is smoothed over the table, the final urn of counted votes is placed at its centre, ready for the announcement...

Still in SLO-MO, the cardinals rise, one by one to their feet, applauding...

A crowd of cardinals are gathered around someone, their backs to us. We PUSH slowly through the crowd, which parts for us, until we reach the cardinal at the centre, the only seated man in the chapel...

Benitez.

Lawrence, having reached him, stares down at the slight figure.

LAWRENCE
(Latin)
< In the name of the whole College of Cardinals, I ask you, Cardinal Benitez, do you accept your canonical election as Supreme Pontiff?>

LAWRENCE
Acceptasne electionem de te canonice factam in Summum Pontificem?

Benitez, as if he hasn't heard, continues to stare down at his feet, his face obscured by a tumbling lock of black hair. A long silence, a collective holding of fearful of breath. If he should refuse...

LAWRENCE (CONT'D)
(Latin)
< Do you accept? >

LAWRENCE (CONT'D)
Acceptasne electionem de te canonice factam in Summum Pontificem?

At last Benitez raises his head and stares at Lawrence.

BENITEZ
(Latin)
< *I accept.* >

BENITEZ
Accepto.

A murmur of relief, of pleasure, erupts around them. Lawrence smiles, pats his heart to indicate his own relief.

LAWRENCE
(Latin)
< *And by what name do you wish to be called?* >

LAWRENCE
Quo nomine vis vocari?

Benitez stands.

BENITEZ
(Latin)
< *Innocent.* >

BENITEZ
Innocentius.

A moment of silence. No Pope has derived a title from one of the virtues for generations. Then applause of approval builds again. Holding the table for support, Lawrence sinks to his knees before the new Holy Father. Benitez stares down at him, smiling, thinking...

INT. SISTINE CHAPEL - DAY / LATER

Lawrence stands with Mandorff preparing the deed of acceptance. Mandorff is filling in Benitez's name on the deed ready for the Pontiff's and witnesses' signatures. Lawrence glances at O'Malley and finds him standing at a table, staring with strange fixity.

LAWRENCE
(amused)
Monsignor, I'm sorry to interrupt you...

O'Malley doesn't react.

LAWRENCE (CONT'D)
Ray...?

Startled, O'Malley looks at him.

LAWRENCE (CONT'D)
I think you should start gathering the cardinal's notes. The sooner we light the stoves, the sooner the world will know we have a new Pope.

O'Malley blinks at him, looking confused, almost frightened.

LAWRENCE (CONT'D)
Are you alright?

MONSIGNOR O'MALLEY
It wasn't... It wasn't the outcome I expected.

LAWRENCE
No. But it's wonderful all the same.

He examines O'Malley, puzzled.

LAWRENCE (CONT'D)
(Quietly)
If it's my position you're worried about, let me reassure you I feel nothing but relief. Our new Holy Father will make a much greater Pope than I ever would have done.

O'Malley nods, a stricken smile. He begins to walk away. Suddenly he wheels around and returns.

MONSIGNOR O'MALLEY
May I speak with you in private?

Lawrence feels a stab of alarm.

INT. SALA REGIA - DAY

The two men stand, alone.

MONSIGNOR O'MALLEY
I'm sorry Your Eminence, I should have told you this morning as soon as I found out, but then...with everything that happened...and I didn't *dream* that Cardinal Benitez would become...

He trails off, helpless .

LAWRENCE
Just tell me what's troubling you.

MONSIGNOR O'MALLEY
I found out... Switzerland. Cardinal Benitez' trip to Switzerland.

LAWRENCE
Switzerland? You mean the hospital in Geneva?

O'Malley looks at him, stricken.

MONSIGNOR O'MALLEY
It wasn't a hospital. It was a clinic.

LAWRENCE
(Beat)
A clinic for what?

INT. SISTINE CHAPEL - DAY

Lawrence strides through the chapel towards the "Room of Tears."

INT. SISTINE CHAPEL - ANTECHAMBER - DAY

He descends the stairs and crosses the sacristy, knocking on the door. Father Haas opens it a little and looks at Lawrence in alarm.

HAAS
His Holiness won't get robed, Your Eminence.

LAWRENCE
If you please, Father Haas...

Haas steps hurriedly aside. Lawrence enters the little room.

INT. SISTINE CHAPEL - ROOM OF TEARS - CONTINUOUS

A pale Benitez sits on a narrow bench in the corner, hunched over, looking small. The PAPAL TAILOR helplessly holds the white cassock of the Pope, not knowing what to do.

LAWRENCE
May I speak to you alone?

BENITEZ
Of course.

The TAILOR puts the cassock away and withdraws.

LAWRENCE
You too, Father.

Surprised, Haas bows and leaves, closing the door behind him. Lawrence and Benitez remain for a moment in silence.

BENITEZ
(ruefully)
It seems that even the smallest vestments are too large... I was waiting for you to come.

LAWRENCE
You must tell me about this treatment at the clinic in Geneva.

He's expecting anger, denial, but Benitez merely smiles, gently.

BENITEZ
Must I, Dean?

LAWRENCE
Yes, you must! Within the hour you will be the most famous man in the world! So tell me - *what is your situation?*

BENITEZ
My "situation," as you call it, is the same as when I was ordained a priest, the same as when I was made a cardinal.

LAWRENCE
But the... *treatment... in Geneva...*

BENITEZ
There was no treatment. I considered it, prayed for guidance. And decided against it.

LAWRENCE
And what would it have been, this treatment?

BENITEZ
It was called a laparoscopic hysterectomy.

A beat. A stunned Lawrence sinks into the nearest chair. After a moment, Benitez pulls up a chair across from him, their knees almost touching.

BENITEZ (CONT'D)
(Gently)
You have to understand, when I was a child, there was no way of knowing my "situation" was more...
(MORE)

BENITEZ (CONT'D)
complicated. I was born to poor parents, in a community where boys were more prized than girls. And the life in the seminary is, as you know, a very modest one. But the truth is, there simply was no reason to think I was different from the other young men. Then, in my late thirties, I had an operation to remove my appendix. And that was when the doctors discovered that I had a uterus and ovaries. My chromosomes would commonly define me as being a woman. And yet I am also... as you see me.

Lawrence stares at him and tries to absorb this. Benitez smiles sympathetically.

BENITEZ (CONT'D)
It was a very dark time for me. I felt as if my entire life as a priest had been lived in a state of sin. Of course, I offered my resignation to the Holy Father. I flew to Rome and told him everything.

LAWRENCE
He *knew?*

BENITEZ
Yes. He knew.

LAWRENCE
And he thought it was acceptable for you to continue as an ordained minister?

BENITEZ
I would assume so. After all, he made me a cardinal *in pectore* in full knowledge of who I am.

Lawrence is baffled, trying to absorb what he has just learned. Benitez gently continues.

BENITEZ (CONT'D)
We considered surgery to have what you might regard as the "female" parts of my body removed. But the night before I was due to fly I realised I was mistaken.
(MORE)

BENITEZ (CONT'D)
I was who I had *always* been. It seemed to me more of a sin to correct His handiwork than to leave my body as it was.

LAWRENCE
Then you... you are still...?

BENITEZ
I am what God made me. And perhaps it is my difference that will make me useful. I think again of your sermon. *I know what it is to exist between the world's certainties.*

Lawrence considers that.

LAWRENCE
Who knows about this, apart from O'Malley?

BENITEZ
Only yourself.

Lawrence nods, thinking that O'Malley can be trusted, that this can be kept secret.

BENITEZ (CONT'D)
And one other of course.

Lawrence looks at him.

BENITEZ (CONT'D)
God.

The two stare at each other.

INT. PAULINE CHAPEL - LATE AFTERNOON

Silence. Lawrence sits, staring blankly ahead, trying to absorb what he has just learned. *Does it fundamentally change who Benitez is?*

He finds himself small in a place so vast, staring at the floor, trying to pray, hoping for guidance, *some sense of connection.* His mind remains numb.

Suddenly he turns and stops, seeing...

<u>A small TURTLE that is working its way across the marble.</u>

Lawrence stares at the surreal sight - this little creature inching towards him.

He walks to the turtle and picks it gently up. There's something so absurd about this.

INT. SISTINE CHAPEL - VESTIBULE - LATE AFTERNOON

O'Malley places ballot papers and notes, any record of the Conclave into the stove and lights them.

Then he activates the chemical canister.

His eyes are drawn slowly up the length of the flue to the point where it projects through the open window and out into the sky.

EXT. VATICAN GROUNDS - LATE AFTERNOON

Lawrence walks back to the fountain and places the turtle gently back into the water.

And then he hears it.

The distant roar of a quarter of a million voices raised in hope and acclamation as they react to the white smoke now rising from the Vatican.

Lawrence listens as the great wave of joy rolls on, and on.

INT. CASA SANTA MARTA - LAWRENCE'S BEDROOM - EVENING

Lawrence packs his clothes and few belongings into his case. Finally he sits, at the same time feeling an overwhelming exhaustion as well as the sensation of having accomplished his task.

He looks up, hearing an electronic whine. The metal shutters at his window are slowly ascending.

He opens the window and looks outside, letting in the air and the sun, as the cool winter breeze plays with the curtains. He smiles, content.

INT. CASA SANTA MARTA - LOBBY - EVENING

The shutters in the lobby rise, letting in the evening light.

INT. CASA SANTA MARTA - BACK OFFICE - EVENING

In the office the canary sits in his cage, reacting to the sound from outside. He begins to quietly chirp.

EXT. STREETS IN ROME - EVENING

Deserted streets in this ancient city. A newspaper in the gutter. An abandoned car on the corner. Next to it an old statue in crumbling marble under the steady stream of a fountain.

I/E. SHOP - STREET NEAR VATICAN - EVENING

The store with the PLASTIC PIETÀS from the beginning. And suddenly there is Cardinal Lawrence, suitcase in hand, resting his gaze on the small statues.

Then he heads down the street and disappears around the corner. We HOLD on the display, the Pietàs, the compassion of the WOMAN cradling the Man of Sorrows.

INT. SALE E TABACCHI - EVENING

A near-empty bar in a small café. On the counter a cold espresso that someone didn't have time to finish.

Behind it, in the background, the faint flicker of a TV. The screen shows the balcony of St. Peter. The red shape of a Cardinal steps through the curtains.

CARDINAL BROTZKUS
Annuntio vobis gaudium magnum.
Habemus Papam!

A small figure in a white cassock steps out next to him, bowing his head in humble submission. And now we hear it, the roar rising to a deafening volume, the sounds of distant celebrations coming through on the TV.

THE END

Made in United States
North Haven, CT
10 April 2025

67818173R00070